DATE DUE

NO 30 '92			
DE 2 '94			
JE 29 '95			
NO 2 '99			

AGING

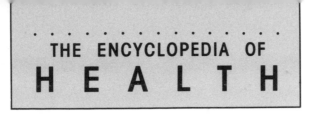

THE ENCYCLOPEDIA OF
HEALTH

THE LIFE CYCLE

Dale C. Garell, M.D. · General Editor

AGING

Edward Edelson

Introduction by C. Everett Koop, M.D., Sc.D.
former Surgeon General, U.S. Public Health Service

CHELSEA HOUSE PUBLISHERS
New York · Philadelphia

ON THE COVER Boy with grandfather

Chelsea House Publishers

EDITOR-IN-CHIEF Remmel Nunn
MANAGING EDITOR Karyn Gullen Browne
COPY CHIEF Juliann Barbato
PICTURE EDITOR Adrian G. Allen
ART DIRECTOR Maria Epes
DEPUTY COPY CHIEF Mark Rifkin
ASSISTANT ART DIRECTOR Noreen Romano
MANUFACTURING MANAGER Gerald Levine
SYSTEMS MANAGER Lindsey Ottman
PRODUCTION MANAGER Joseph Romano
PRODUCTION COORDINATOR Marie Claire Cebrián

The Encyclopedia of Health
SENIOR EDITOR Jake Goldberg

Staff for AGING

ASSISTANT EDITOR Nicole Bowen
COPY EDITOR Philip Koslow
EDITORIAL ASSISTANT Leigh Hope Wood
PICTURE RESEARCHER Georganne M. Backman
SENIOR DESIGNER Marjorie Zaum
DESIGN ASSISTANT Debora Smith

Library of Congress Cataloging-in-Publication Data

Edelson, Edward
    Aging/by Edward Edelson.
        p. cm.—(The Encyclopedia of health)
    Includes bibliographical references.
    Summary: Surveys issues dealing with the process of aging, including the difference
between generations in both physical and mental capacities and the treatment of the
elderly.
    ISBN 0-7910-0035-4
        0-7910-0475-9 (pbk.)
    1. Aging—Juvenile literature. [1. Aging. 2. Old age.]
I. Title. II. Series   90-1722
QP86.E24 1990   CIP
612.6'7—dc20   AC

CONTENTS

The goal of the ENCYCLOPEDIA OF HEALTH *is to provide general information in the ever-changing areas of physiology, psychology, and related medical issues. The titles in this series are not intended to take the place of the professional advice of a physician or other health care professional.*

THE ENCYCLOPEDIA OF
H E A L T H

THE HEALTHY BODY

The Circulatory System
Dental Health
The Digestive System
The Endocrine System
Exercise
Genetics & Heredity
The Human Body: An Overview
Hygienc
The Immune System
Memory & Learning
The Musculoskeletal System
The Nervous System
Nutrition
The Reproductive System
The Respiratory System
The Senses
Speech & Hearing
Sports Medicine
Vision
Vitamins & Minerals

THE LIFE CYCLE

Adolescence
Adulthood
Aging
Childhood
Death & Dying
The Family
Friendship & Love
Pregnancy & Birth

MEDICAL ISSUES

Careers in Health Care
Environmental Health
Folk Medicine
Health Care Delivery
Holistic Medicine
Medical Ethics
Medical Fakes & Frauds
Medical Technology
Medicine & the Law
Occupational Health
Public Health

PSYCHOLOGICAL DISORDERS
AND THEIR TREATMENT

Anxiety & Phobias
Child Abuse
Compulsive Behavior
Delinquency & Criminal Behavior
Depression
Diagnosing & Treating Mental Illness
Eating Habits & Disorders
Learning Disabilities
Mental Retardation
Personality Disorders
Schizophrenia
Stress Management
Suicide

MEDICAL DISORDERS
AND THEIR TREATMENT

AIDS
Allergies
Alzheimer's Disease
Arthritis
Birth Defects
Cancer
The Common Cold
Diabetes
Emergency Medicine & First Aid
Gynecological Disorders
Headaches
The Hospital
Kidney Disorders
Medical Diagnosis
The Mind-Body Connection
Mononucleosis and Other Infectious Diseases
Nuclear Medicine
Organ Transplants
Pain
Physical Handicaps
Poisons & Toxins
Prescription & OTC Drugs
Sexually Transmitted Diseases
Skin Disorders
Stroke & Heart Disease
Substance Abuse
Tropical Medicine

PREVENTION AND EDUCATION: THE KEYS TO GOOD HEALTH

C. Everett Koop, M.D., Sc.D.
former Surgeon General,
U.S. Public Health Service

The issue of health education has received particular attention in recent years because of the presence of AIDS in the news. But our response to this particular tragedy points up a number of broader issues that doctors, public health officials, educators, and the public face. In particular, it points up the necessity for sound health education for citizens of all ages.

Over the past 25 years this country has been able to bring about dramatic declines in the death rates for heart disease, stroke, accidents, and, for people under the age of 45, cancer. Today, Americans generally eat better and take better care of themselves than ever before. Thus, with the help of modern science and technology, they have a better chance of surviving serious—even catastrophic—illnesses. That's the good news.

But, like every phonograph record, there's a flip side, and one with special significance for young adults. According to a report issued in 1979 by Dr. Julius Richmond, my predecessor as Surgeon General, Americans aged 15 to 24 had a higher death rate in 1979 than they did 20 years earlier. The causes: violent death and injury, alcohol and drug abuse, unwanted pregnancies, and sexually transmitted diseases. Adolescents are particularly vulnerable because they are beginning to explore their own sexuality and perhaps to experiment with drugs. The need for educating young people is critical, and the price of neglect is high.

Yet even for the population as a whole, our health is still far from what it could be. Why? A 1974 Canadian government report attributed all death and disease to four broad elements: inadequacies in the health care system, behavioral factors or unhealthy life-styles, environmental hazards, and human biological factors.

To be sure, there are diseases that are still beyond the control of even our advanced medical knowledge and techniques. And despite yearnings that are as old as the human race itself, there is no "fountain of youth" to ward off aging and death. Still, there is a solution to many of the problems that undermine sound health. In a word, that solution is prevention. Prevention, which includes health promotion and education, saves lives, improves the quality of life, and, in the long run, saves money.

In the United States, organized public health activities and preventive medicine have a long history. Important milestones include the improvement of sanitary procedures and the development of pasteurized milk in the late 19th century, and the introduction in the mid-20th century of effective vaccines against polio, measles, German measles, mumps, and other once-rampant diseases. Internationally, organized public health efforts began on a wide-scale basis with the International Sanitary Conference of 1851, to which 12 nations sent representatives. The World Health Organization, founded in 1948, continues these efforts under the aegis of the United Nations, with particular emphasis on combatting communicable diseases and the training of health care workers.

Despite these accomplishments, much remains to be done in the field of prevention. For too long, we have had a medical care system that is science- and technology-based, focused, essentially, on illness and mortality. It is now patently obvious that both the social and the economic costs of such a system are becoming insupportable.

Implementing prevention—and its corollaries, health education and promotion—is the job of several groups of people.

First, the medical and scientific professions need to continue basic scientific research, and here we are making considerable progress. But increased concern with prevention will also have a decided impact on how primary care doctors practice medicine. With a shift to health-based rather than morbidity-based medicine, the role of the "new physician" will include a healthy dose of patient education.

Second, practitioners of the social and behavioral sciences—psychologists, economists, city planners—along with lawyers, business leaders, and government officials—must solve the practical and ethical dilemmas confronting us: poverty, crime, civil rights, literacy, education, employment, housing, sanitation, environmental protection, health care delivery systems, and so forth. All of these issues affect public health.

Third is the public at large. We'll consider that very important group in a moment.

Fourth, and the linchpin in this effort, is the public health profession—doctors, epidemiologists, teachers—who must harness the professional expertise of the first two groups and the common sense and cooperation of the third, the public. They must define the problems statistically and qualitatively and then help us set priorities for finding the solutions.

To a very large extent, improving those statistics is the responsibility of every individual. So let's consider more specifically what the role of the individual should be and why health education is so important to that role. First, and most obviously, individuals can protect themselves from illness and injury and thus minimize their need for professional medical care. They can eat nutritious food, get adequate exercise, avoid tobacco, alcohol, and drugs, and take prudent steps to avoid accidents. The proverbial "apple a day keeps the doctor away" is not so far from the truth, after all.

Second, individuals should actively participate in their own medical care. They should schedule regular medical and dental checkups. Should they develop an illness or injury, they should know when to treat themselves and when to seek professional help. To gain the maximum benefit from any medical treatment that they do require, individuals must become partners in that treatment. For instance, they should understand the effects and side effects of medications. I counsel young physicians that there is no such thing as too much information when talking with patients. But the corollary is the patient must know enough about the nuts and bolts of the healing process to understand what the doctor is telling him. That is at least partially the patient's responsibility.

Education is equally necessary for us to understand the ethical and public policy issues in health care today. Sometimes individuals will encounter these issues in making decisions about their own treatment or that of family members. Other citizens may encounter them as jurors in medical malpractice cases. But we all become involved, indirectly, when we elect our public officials, from school board members to the president. Should surrogate parenting be legal? To what extent is drug testing desirable, legal, or necessary? Should there be public funding for family planning, hospitals, various types of medical research, and medical care for the indigent? How should we allocate scant technological resources, such as kidney dialysis and organ transplants? What is the proper role of government in protecting the rights of patients?

What are the broad goals of public health in the United States today? In 1980, the Public Health Service issued a report aptly entitled *Promoting Health—Preventing Disease: Objectives for the Nation*. This report expressed its goals in terms of mortality and in terms of intermediate goals in education and health improvement. It identified 15 major concerns: controlling high blood pressure; improving family planning; improving pregnancy care and infant health; increasing the rate of immunization; controlling sexually transmitted diseases; controlling the presence of toxic agents and radiation in the environment; improving occupational safety and health; preventing accidents; promoting water fluoridation and dental health; controlling infectious diseases; decreasing smoking; decreasing alcohol and drug abuse; improving nutrition; promoting physical fitness and exercise; and controlling stress and violent behavior.

For healthy adolescents and young adults (ages 15 to 24), the specific goal was a 20% reduction in deaths, with a special focus on motor vehicle injuries and alcohol and drug abuse. For adults (ages 25 to 64), the aim was 25% fewer deaths, with a concentration on heart attacks, strokes, and cancers.

Smoking is perhaps the best example of how individual behavior can have a direct impact on health. Today cigarette smoking is recognized as the most important single preventable cause of death in our society. It is responsible for more cancers and more cancer deaths than any other known agent; is a prime risk factor for heart and blood vessel disease, chronic bronchitis, and emphysema; and is a frequent cause of complications in pregnancies and of babies born prematurely, underweight, or with potentially fatal respiratory and cardiovascular problems.

Since the release of the Surgeon General's first report on smoking in 1964, the proportion of adult smokers has declined substantially, from 43% in 1965 to 30.5% in 1985. Since 1965, 37 million people have quit smoking. Although there is still much work to be done if we are to become a "smoke-free society," it is heartening to note that public health and public education efforts—such as warnings on cigarette packages and bans on broadcast advertising—have already had significant effects.

In 1835, Alexis de Tocqueville, a French visitor to America, wrote, "In America the passion for physical well-being is general." Today, as then, health and fitness are front-page items. But with the greater scientific and technological resources now available to us, we are in a far stronger position to make good health care available to everyone. And with the greater technological threats to us as we approach the 21st century, the need to do so is more urgent than ever before. Comprehensive information about basic biology, preventive medicine, medical and surgical treatments, and related ethical and public policy issues can help you arm yourself with the knowledge you need to be healthy throughout your life.

FOREWORD

Dale C. Garell, M.D.

Advances in our understanding of health and disease during the 20th century have been truly remarkable. Indeed, it could be argued that modern health care is one of the greatest accomplishments in all of human history. In the early 1900s, improvements in sanitation, water treatment, and sewage disposal reduced death rates and increased longevity. Previously untreatable illnesses can now be managed with antibiotics, immunizations, and modern surgical techniques. Discoveries in the fields of immunology, genetic diagnosis, and organ transplantation are revolutionizing the prevention and treatment of disease. Modern medicine is even making inroads against cancer and heart disease, two of the leading causes of death in the United States.

Although there is much to be proud of, medicine continues to face enormous challenges. Science has vanquished diseases such as smallpox and polio, but new killers, most notably AIDS, confront us. Moreover, we now victimize ourselves with what some have called "diseases of choice," or those brought on by drug and alcohol abuse, bad eating habits, and mismanagement of the stresses and strains of contemporary life. The very technology that is doing so much to prolong life has brought with it previously unimaginable ethical dilemmas related to issues of death and dying. The rising cost of health care is a matter of central concern to us all. And violence in the form of automobile accidents, homicide, and suicide remains the major killer of young adults.

In the past, most people were content to leave health care and medical treatment in the hands of professionals. But since the 1960s, the consumer of medical care—that is, the patient—has assumed an increasingly central role in the management of his or her own health. There has also been a new emphasis placed on prevention: People are recognizing that their own actions can help prevent many of the conditions that have caused death and disease in the past. This accounts for the growing commitment to good nutrition and regular exercise, for the fact that more and more people are choosing not to smoke, and for a new moderation in people's drinking habits.

People want to know more about themselves and their own health. They are curious about their body: its anatomy, physiology, and biochemistry. They want to keep up with rapidly evolving medical technologies and procedures. They are willing to educate themselves about common disorders and diseases so that they can be full partners in their own health care.

The ENCYCLOPEDIA OF HEALTH is designed to provide the basic knowledge that readers will need if they are to take significant responsibility for their own health. It is also meant to serve as a frame of reference for further study and exploration. The ENCYCLOPEDIA is divided into five subsections: The Healthy Body; the Life Cycle; Medical Disorders & Their Treatment; Psychological Disorders & Their Treatment; and Medical Issues. For each topic covered by the ENCYCLOPEDIA, we present the essential facts about the relevant biology; the symptoms, diagnosis, and treatment of common diseases and disorders; and ways in which you can prevent or reduce the severity of health problems when that is possible. The ENCYCLOPEDIA also projects what may lie ahead in the way of future treatment or prevention strategies.

The broad range of topics and issues covered in the ENCYCLOPEDIA reflects the fact that human health encompasses physical, psychological, social, environmental, and spiritual well-being. Just as the mind and the body are inextricably linked, so, too, is the individual an integral part of the wider world that comprises his or her family, society, and environment. To discuss health in its broadest aspect it is necessary to explore the many ways in which it is connected to such fields as law, social science, public policy, economics, and even religion. And so, the ENCYCLOPEDIA is meant to be a bridge between science, medical technology, the world at large, and you. I hope that it will inspire you to pursue in greater depth particular areas of interest and that you will take advantage of the suggestions for further reading and the lists of resources and organizations that can provide additional information.

CHAPTER 1

AGING
AMERICA

The first chapter of Ivan Turgenev's 1862 novel, *Fathers and Sons*, introduces Nicholas Petrovich Kirsanov, one of the fathers in the title. He is described as advanced in years, a "grizzled, slightly bent, stoutish, elderly gentleman." Nicholas Petrovich Kirsanov is 41 years old.

Turgenev's novel illustrates just how much ideas of old age have changed since the 19th century. In his day, 41 was the beginning of old age. Today, it is almost the prime of life. People have come to expect not only a much longer life span but also a healthier one than did people of the 19th century—or indeed any other century before it. People today are living in a revolutionary era in regard to aging.

AN OLDER POPULATION

The United States has customarily regarded itself as a young nation. In fact, its accent in recent years has been changing subtly away from youth. The American population is growing older. The median age of Americans today is 32. It is projected to rise to 36 by the year 2000 and to 42 by 2040. By then, a fifth of all Americans will be 65 or older.

And so, quite rightly, aging has become a major concern of science, medicine, and government. Science focuses on the basic mechanisms of aging. Medicine looks at the ailments of aging and how they can be treated and prevented. Government tries to cope with the new demands of an older population.

The increase in the number of older people is due partly to a general advance in living conditions and partly to medical progress. Better nutrition, housing, and working conditions mean that more people live longer and stay fit longer. To give just one example, American men who are the same age as Nicholas Petrovich Kirsanov now sometimes play professional sports, which are not games for old men.

The conquest through vaccination and antibiotic treatment of the infectious diseases, such as polio and tuberculosis, that were the major killers at the turn of the century has also had a major impact in prolonging life and fitness—not only by the virtual elimination of childhood diseases in developed countries but also by making death from infectious disease rare at any age (with the painful exception of *acquired immune deficiency syndrome* [AIDS], which has no cure at this time). Progress is also being made in the fight against diseases that take many years to develop. Notably, the age-adjusted death rate from heart disease has been reduced by a third since the 1950s, while the death rate from stroke has been halved.

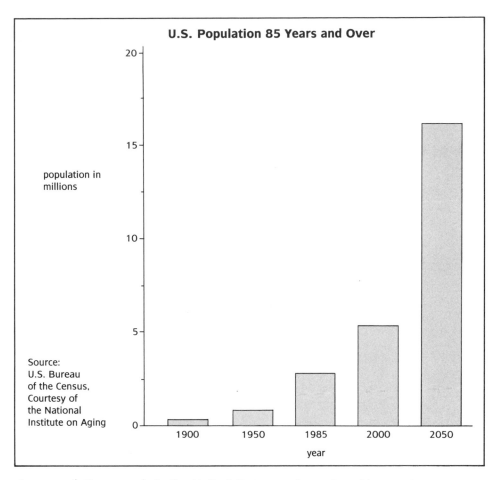

U.S. Population 85 Years and Over

population in millions

Source:
U.S. Bureau
of the Census,
Courtesy of
the National
Institute on Aging

year

As a population, people in the United States are becoming older. Projections show that by the year 2000 more than 5 million Americans will be 85 or older; there will be more than 15 million by 2050.

In most respects, these developments are regarded as good news. A long, healthy life is obviously preferred to death from illness at an early age. In some respects, however, society is poorly equipped to handle the problems and complexities that come with this sort of progress. To give one example in the socioeconomic sphere, retirement today is something quite different than it was at the beginning of the century.

In 1900, the average American man spent most of his life working and a relatively brief time—two or three years—in retirement. In 1980, the average man could expect to spend nearly 14 years, close to a fifth of his entire life span, in retirement. The prolongation of retirement has raised several issues. One is financial: How can older people pay their bills for all those years? Another is the issue of retirement itself—whether the traditional age of retirement should be changed from 65. Yet another is a social issue: How can the retirement years be made productive and enjoyable for both those who want to continue working and those who do not?

Statistics show that most Americans prefer to retire early. A Louis Harris study in 1979 found that almost two-thirds of retirees had left work before age 65. Only 5% had found other full-time jobs, and 8% were working part-time. Department of Labor statistics from 1985 showed that only 25% of men and 14% of women over 65 were still working. Only 10% of men and 4% of women 70 and over were still in the work force.

But there is a trend to make it easier for older people to remain at work. Mandatory retirement at age 65 or 70, once common, is now illegal in most industries. And as the number of teenagers declines because of lower birth rates after the so-called baby boom years, employers are turning to older people as an alternative source of labor. Fast-food chains, which traditionally have hired teenagers for relatively low-paying part-time jobs, have begun to hire retirees to fill the gap.

Economically, the picture is mixed. In 1986, the median income for families headed by people 65 or older was only 60% of the income of younger families. And income distribution is much more unequal among the elderly than among the nonelderly. In 1987, Census Bureau figures showed that 28% of those 65 and over lived at or near the poverty level, compared to 22% of younger people. The percentage would have been even higher if not for regular increases in Social Security payments, which made up for a decline in other sources of income. Yet older people tend to have relatively high assets—the savings of a lifetime. The Census Bureau in 1984 found the median net worth of people 65 and over to be $60,266, compared to $35,581 for the 35 to 44 age group. But *home equity*, the worth of one's house, accounted for more than two-thirds of the assets of the elderly, leaving little in *liquid assets*, money that can be spent.

One crucial economic statistic is that there is only one budget category in which older people spend more than the young—health care. In 1984, people under 65 spent 3% of their income on health care. Those between 65 and 74 spent 8% of their income on health care. For those 75 and over, it was 13%. A third of all U.S. health care spending is for the elderly, and the percentage is increasing.

These issues become more intense as the number of older people grows. Whereas in 1900 only 1 American in 25 was 65 or older, in 1990 the ratio was 1 in 8. The older population has been growing more than twice as fast as the rest of the population

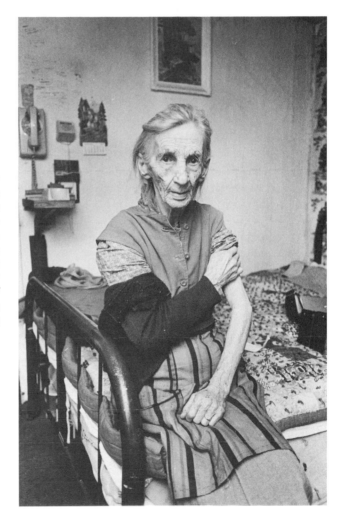

Although many older people may own a home or have savings, they tend to have less money available for living expenses than do the young. Census Bureau figures from 1987 showed that 28% of those 65 and older were living at or near the poverty level.

since the 1960s, and the fastest growth has been in the oldest group of Americans. By the year 2000, half the elderly population will be 75 or older. By 2050, the 85-plus population will have increased 7-fold, to 16 million, if current projections are correct.

This trend is common to the industrialized nations but not to the developing countries of Africa, Asia, and South and Central America. These countries have young populations, in large part because they have high birth rates. In the United States, Europe, and Japan, birth rates have declined. Several developed countries, West Germany among them, have experienced a decrease in population, with fewer births than deaths. The proportion of the population over 65 in these countries is expected to double in the next 40 years, which means that a fifth of their population will be 65 or over.

The steady growth in the number of older people has thrust aging to the forefront of public, medical, and scientific concern. As individuals, people are concerned because they expect to live in the new era of aging. And society as a whole has learned the magnitude of the problems that must be solved. To give just one example, almost no research was done on *Alzheimer's disease*, the major cause of mental deterioration in old age, before the 1980s. It is now a major focus of scientific and medical research because an estimated 2.5 million Americans, most of them elderly, suffer the irreversible mental degeneration caused by Alzheimer's disease.

THE STUDY OF AGING

Gerontology, the scientific study of aging, and *geriatrics*, the branch of medicine concerned with aging, are both relatively young. Scientifically, says Dr. Nathan Shock, former director of the National Institute on Aging's Gerontology Research Center, aging studies were barren until relatively recently. "A large share of the literature on aging was devoted to descriptions of techniques for prolonging life in humans," he said.

> These nostrums ranged from special diets to the administration of hormones, including transplantation of testicular tissue from animals (goats and apes) to humans. Controlled studies were never conducted,

although glowing accounts of rejuvenating effects constituted a large part of the so-called scientific literature on aging.

The field began to change in 1974, with the establishment by the U.S. Congress of the National Institute on Aging "for the conduct and support of biomedical, social and behavioral research and training related to the aging process." Dr. Shock became director of the institute's Gerontology Research Center in Baltimore, Maryland, where systematic research is being done on the aging process.

One of the center's major efforts is the Baltimore Longitudinal Study of Aging, which began in 1958, even before the National Institute on Aging was founded. It is the first effort to study the changes that occur in healthy individuals as they grow older. More than 1,000 people have volunteered for the program. Each checks into the center every two years for two and a half days of physical examinations, tests of memory and learning abilities, and questioning about social and behavioral patterns. A great deal of the information available today about normal aging comes from the Longitudinal Study of Aging.

The study does not give a complete picture, however, because its subjects are a *self-selected* group. Researchers doing studies on volunteers—those who select themselves to participate rather than being chosen randomly—need to consider the characteristics of those likely to volunteer and how these characteristics might influence the findings. Most subjects of the Longitudinal Study of Aging are well-to-do white residents of the Baltimore area. More recently, the National Institute on Aging has started a long-term study that will follow 14,000 Americans as they grow older. Four groups are being studied: working-class people in Boston; residents of New Haven, Connecticut; small-town residents in rural Iowa; and a representative sample of older people from both rural and urban areas of North Carolina. The first report from this project, whose cumbersome title is *Established Populations for Epidemiological Studies of the Elderly*, was issued in 1986. It gave *baseline data* (data at the start of the study against which later data will be compared) for the people being studied. Reports on the medical and social conditions of the groups will be published periodically for many years.

Maintaining healthy habits throughout the years can do much to increase life span. Regular exercise is important no matter how old a person is. This woman leads an exercise class for senior citizens in Miami, Florida.

Such studies demonstrate how the focus of gerontology has changed. In its early days, the handful of researchers in the field concentrated their efforts on the discovery of the cause of aging, with the goal of developing some method that could slow or reverse the aging process. Those efforts were essentially fruitless. Science does not know the cause of aging, and efforts to develop an elixir of youth remain mostly speculative. The basic aim now is to get a better understanding of the normal aging process so as to minimize the damage that occurs with age.

There are two conflicting theories about aging. One is that it is inevitably accompanied by an increasing burden of illness, both mental and physical: The older people become, the sicker they become. Medical statistics seem to bear out this pessimistic view; the incidence of most chronic diseases, from arthritis to cancer, rises sharply with age.

An opposing theory is that much of this damage is preventable. Dr. John W. Rowe, a former director of the National Institute on Aging, notes that international studies show different patterns of aging in industrialized societies, such as the United States, as compared to more traditional rural societies. "It is at least a reasonable hypothesis, given such cross-cultural differences, that attributions of change to age per se may often be exaggerated and that factors of diet, exercise, nutrition and the like may have been underestimated or ignored as potential moderators of the aging process," Dr. Rowe said. "If so, the prospects for avoidance or even reversal of functional loss with age are vastly improved, and thus the risk of adverse health outcomes reduced."

One major factor that is often overlooked, Dr. Rowe says, is that studies deal with averages, whereas every person ages differently. A project such as the Longitudinal Study of Aging finds that on the average older people suffer substantial losses in physical function as they age. But within the group can be found individuals who have suffered little or no loss. Studies of those individuals could develop techniques for reducing physical and mental losses for all older people, Dr. Rowe maintains.

The goal of research in the 1990s is not so much to extend the average life span as to keep people healthier for a longer time. That goal is often expressed in the form of a graph showing mortality as a function of age. Such a graph of 19th-century data shows a line with a regular downward slope, as disease caused steady attrition. A similar graph today shows an almost rectangular slope, with fewer deaths in the years before old age, followed by a rapid drop. Gerontologists speak of an ideal "rectangular curve," achievable through conquest of all the major chronic diseases. That ideal curve would show only minor attrition from illness and accident until the age of 80 or over, followed by an almost perpendicular drop representing death caused not by specific diseases but by old age, a wearing out of the body systems.

Are sickness and disability an inevitable part of old age? Or can the major diseases that go with aging be eliminated? The answers depend on the fundamental cause of aging, about which there are many theories.

This book will examine mainly the scientific, biological aspects of aging. Growing old also brings to a person a range of emotional and social changes. People deal with these in their own way. They learn to relate to their children and grandchildren; learn to cope with the death of spouses, friends, and relatives; and try to understand the changes in themselves and in the world around them. Understanding the biology behind the physical changes brought about by age may enable the elderly to better come to terms with these emotional difficulties. It may also help the young to better understand what an elderly person is experiencing.

•   •   •   •

CHAPTER 2

THEORIES OF AGING

Ponce de León's search for the fountain of youth

The quest for the fountain of youth, the magic formula that will keep a person young forever, is as old as humanity and as new as headlines in today's supermarket tabloids. One of the oldest stories ever told, found on 12 tablets in the palace of Ashurbanipal, a king who ruled Assyria more than 2,000 years ago, tells how the legendary king Gilgamesh sought a flower of immortality. Today, stories of idyllic places where people are said to live for 150 years or more—Vilcabamba in Ecuador, Hunza in Asia, the Abkhaz Republic in the Caucasus region of the Soviet Union—are read with fascination. Books peddling one regimen or another for prolonging youth and life sell briskly.

Yet there is no proven fountain of youth, in large part because science does not know the cause of aging. Scientists know that humans, like other species, have a limited life span; they do not know the underlying mechanism that makes people grow old and die. A vigorous program of basic research on aging has gone on for decades, but scientists are no closer now to an understanding of the molecular processes of aging than they were in the 1960s. What they do have is a growing realization of the complexity of the problem.

A few decades ago, some scientists thought they could discover a single biological mechanism that makes animals grow old. That idea has mostly been abandoned. The prevailing belief now is that aging is the result of a complex set of processes working in combination. Researchers today have a number of theories about the nature of these mechanisms of aging.

Theories of aging fall into two general categories. One assumes that aging is caused by the accumulated damage that occurs as the years go by; errors pile up until they become fatal. The other says that organisms grow old because aging is programmed into the basic *molecules* of life. (A molecule is a combination of two or more atoms joined to form the smallest part of a substance that will retain that substance's unique properties.)

Both *error theories* and *programming theories* of aging focus on the essential machinery of the living *cell*—the fundamental unit of living organisms. They start with *deoxyribonucleic acid* (DNA), the molecule that resides in the nucleus of the living cell and carries the genetic information required for life and reproduction. DNA is a long, thin molecule made up of four building blocks called *nucleotides*. Every cell in the human body has about 3 billion nucleotides of DNA, containing the information for perhaps 100,000 *genes*. Each gene codes for the production of one *protein*—one of a group of compounds that compose muscle tissue, antibodies, hormones, and many other bodily components. These proteins carry out all the functions of living cells. Error theories say that as time goes by, the production of proteins by DNA or the ability of proteins to do their jobs (or both) diminishes.

ERROR THEORIES

The *wear and tear theory* states that aging occurs because the efficiency of the body's repair mechanisms for DNA declines over the years. DNA suffers continuous damage for a variety of reasons, and each cell has proteins that repair the damage. Some scientists believe that this repair system starts to fall behind with time, allowing DNA errors to accumulate until they become fatal. New laboratory techniques that allow biologists to directly measure DNA damage and repair are being used to test this theory.

A variation on that theme is the *error catastrophe theory*, proposed by Leslie Orgel of the Salk Institute in San Diego, which says that cumulative damage to the protein-making mechanisms builds up until a crisis point is reached. When the level of errors reaches a critical threshold, there is a domino effect, in which malfunction of one protein affects other proteins until the cell— and ultimately the organism—dies.

A different set of error theories looks at protein function rather than DNA-governed protein production. One theory focuses on highly unstable chemical fragments called *free radicals*, which are produced in the body during the process of *metabolism*— conversion of food and oxygen into the energy the body needs. Free radicals combine readily with all other molecules, so cells have effective ways of removing them as they are formed. The *free radical theory* of aging says that the removal process is not good enough and that damage done by the reaction of free radicals with essential molecules in the cells eventually degrades the functioning of vital cell molecules, such as proteins.

The free radical theory has been tested in various ways, generally by use of *antioxidant chemicals* (substances that inhibit reactions promoted by oxygen) that are efficient scavengers of free radicals. Vitamins C and E are antioxidants. Some animal experiments have found increased life span with regular doses of vitamin E and other antioxidants. Most have not. A confounding issue is that large doses of vitamin E can reduce the body's production of other antioxidants. Animals given large doses of vitamin E in experiments also lose a lot of weight. Weight loss alone can extend longevity of laboratory animals. The free radical theory of aging remains popular in best-selling books and supermarket tabloids, but it is highly controversial among scientists.

Some free radical studies have centered on *lipofuscin*, a dark *pigment* (bodily coloring matter) that accumulates in cells with age. Some scientists believe that lipofuscin causes aging damage because it interferes with essential cell functions. A drug called *centrophenoxine*, which reduces accumulation of lipofuscin, has been used in both animal and human aging experiments. Those tests have produced no clear evidence that centrophenoxine can slow the aging process.

The *cross-linking theory* is based on the belief that aging results from chemical bonds called *cross-links* between protein molecules. Cross-linking is said to be particularly important in regard to *collagen*, the protein that is an essential *matrix* (intercellular structural) material in *tendons* (fibrous cords that attach bone to muscle), *cartilage* (specialized fibrous connective tissue), bone, and skin. Skin becomes less flexible with age because of cross-linking, and the theory says that the same process goes on in other proteins, causing the changes known as aging. However, studies of cross-linking and aging have been inconclusive.

One more error theory, proposed by Leo Szilard, a physicist who was instrumental in the development of the atom bomb and who went into biological research late in life, attributes aging to *somatic mutations*. A mutation is a change in DNA caused by *radiation* (energy carried by waves of such things as light, electrons, or other subatomic particles), chemicals, or mistakes in duplicating the DNA molecule. Mutations that occur in reproductive cells—egg or sperm—can cause birth defects and genetic diseases. The *somatic mutation theory* explains aging as an accumulation of mutations in the DNA contained in the nonreproductive, or somatic, cells of the body. When enough mutations accumulate, a cell dies, Szilard proposed; when enough cells die, the organism dies.

Then there is the *metabolic rate theory* of aging, which says that organisms that live faster die faster. Proponents point to the undisputed fact that smaller animals such as mice, which have faster metabolic rates than larger animals such as humans, also have a much shorter life span. There is some experimental evidence to support this point of view. Thus far, the only laboratory intervention that has successfully extended the life span of animals is *calorie restriction*—semistarvation, a measure that reduces the amount of metabolic activity. In 1935, a scientist

One theory of aging states that cross-linking occurs between protein molecules in the body. This affects the protein in the skin, which becomes less flexible with age because of these cross-links.

named Clive McCay at Cornell University showed that the life span of mice could be increased by half if they were fed just enough calories to provide them with basic nutritional needs. The mice not only lived longer but also suffered fewer of the diseases that come with aging.

McCay's experiment has been repeated many times with mice and with rats, showing similar results. Until recently, however, it had not been tried in higher animals. At this writing, the National Institute on Aging is conducting a calorie restriction study with monkeys, which are relatively close relatives of humans, to see whether it affects their life span. For obvious reasons, no one is thinking of a similar experiment with humans. Although malnutrition is unhappily a common human experience, it is not the same as calorie restriction. The difference is that malnutrition does not give an adequate supply of basic nutrients, whereas calorie restriction does. Starving humans do not live long because the lack of essential nutrients weakens the body. Whether systematic caloric restriction throughout life could make humans live longer may never be known.

Error theories of aging raise the possibility of major extensions of the life span: If errors can be prevented or corrected, people will live longer. The belief that aging is programmed in the genes does not allow for that possibility. It says nature has built into the genes a limit on the life span of all species.

PROGRAMMING THEORIES

There do seem to be definite limits to life spans. A mouse can be made to live for 3 years rather than 2, but it will not live for 10 years. The age limit for humans is not much more than a century; the longest verified life span of any human is 120 years. Stories of people living to 140 or 150 invariably come from remote places like Hunza or the Caucasus, where dates of births and deaths are haphazardly recorded, where children often adopt the names of parents, and where people can start looking very old at relatively young ages. Claims of extreme longevity in these far-off places have not been verified by careful scientific studies.

One major discovery in the area of programmed aging was made in the 1960s at the Wistar Institute in Philadelphia by Leonard Hayflick and Paul Moorhead, who were growing cells in laboratory culture. Given adequate nutrition, cells will readily reproduce by doubling—but only to a point, Hayflick and Moorhead found. For human cells, the point is about 50 doublings. For mice, it is correspondingly less. No laboratory manipulation will induce normal cells to reproduce beyond what seems to be a preset limit. The exception is cancer. Malignant cells achieve a grim immortality, doubling and redoubling without limit.

If human aging is programmed by nature, what is the ultimate control mechanism? The answer almost certainly would lie somewhere in the genes. It is possible that nature has designed the cells' genes to work for only a limited time and that when that time comes, they stop. It is also possible that the master control lies in the genes of one organ system or another. Researchers have examined two systems, the *endocrine system* and the *immune system*. The endocrine system comprises the *hormones*—

chemicals that regulate certain processes or alter certain organs—and the organs that secrete them. The immune system is composed of antibodies and special cells that fight bacteria, viruses, and other harmful foreign bodies.

As well as defending the body against infectious agents, the immune system plays a role in defending against cancer, whose incidence rises steadily with age in all species. One important organ of the immune system is the *thymus*, located in the chest. The thymus is the organ in which several kinds of important immune system cells reach maturity. The thymus has a limited life. It reaches its maximum size during the teen years in humans and then shrivels away over several decades. Corresponding changes in immune function have been detected. Immune function declines with age to a third or less of its peak power in youth.

The age limit for humans seems to be close to a century; 120 years is the longest verified life span. This woman, who was born the daughter of a slave, is shown here the day before her 112th birthday in 1985.

Some scientists think that aging is caused by the programmed decline of the genes that control immune defenses.

Other scientists believe that the glands that control the endocrine system control aging. The master control of the endocrine system consists of the *hypothalamus,* a part of the brain that secretes hormones that govern the *pituitary gland,* which sits just below it. Pituitary hormones circulate throughout the body, governing the glands that secrete other essential hormones. A theory held by researchers such as Roy Walford of the University of Southern California is that the hypothalamus is pro-

This photomicrograph shows vitamin C magnified 63 times. Vitamin C and many other substances have been falsely sold as cures for aging. Although this vitamin is needed for good health, it cannot stop the aging process.

grammed to instruct the pituitary to release a so-called death hormone at the appropriate time of life. No evidence that a death hormone exists has yet been found, however.

Some endocrine events are clearly related to age—most notably *menopause* in women. Menopause is the period during which production of the sex hormone *estrogen* stops. In 1989, scientists reported that the life span in women was related to the age at which menopause begins, with early menopause being associated with a shorter life span. That finding, however, does not apply to men because there is no clear-cut male menopause comparable to what happens in women. The relationship between endocrine system function and aging is still unclear.

Indeed, a review of theories of aging reveals that the evidence for all of them is rickety or nonexistent. Biologists have brought increasingly more powerful laboratory techniques to bear on the issue in the past few decades. They have looked at DNA, proteins, and other cell components with all the tools made available by advances such as *genetic engineering*—in which DNA is cut and recombined at specific spots by *enzymes* (substances that initiate or speed a reaction). However, they are no closer now than they ever were to understanding the mechanism of aging.

That fact has not stopped hucksters from promoting sure "cures" for aging—vitamin E, vitamin C, proteins, enzymes, *amino acids* (components of protein), alone or in combination, are hawked as products that will let people stay young forever. The sales pitch is to describe studies in which one substance or another has produced positive results while ignoring all the negative studies. Any assessment of these products has to come back to one essential point: There is no solid scientific proof for any of them.

These decades of research may seem unproductive, but in fact they have clarified a number of issues and given scientists a new set of goals. Twenty years ago, the goal of most researchers was to extend the life span so that people would live to 150 or 200. Today the goal is to keep people healthy longer—"to put more life into years, not more years into life," as one researcher said. The idea is to keep the body and the mind working better as the years go by.

•   •   •   •

CHAPTER 3

AGING:
THE BODY

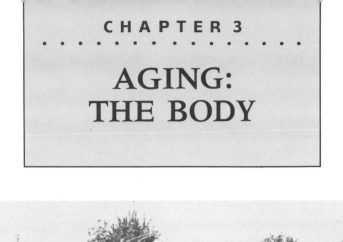

Eighty-year-old man running a 3,000-meter race

$\mathbf{E}$veryone knows—or thinks they know—what happens to the human body with age: All the parts deteriorate, and function declines. To some extent, that picture is accurate. Studies that look at large numbers of people as they grow older find an overall decline in a number of body systems and an increase in chronic diseases—heart attacks, arthritis, diabetes, cancer, and many more. Stamina is reduced, reflexes get slower, the heart pumps blood less efficiently, and so on. But this image of overall decline and increasing illness with age is not as gloomy as it seems.

REDUCING PHYSICAL AGING

Older people must be considered one at a time, not as a group. There is tremendous variability in the way people age. For example, some 80-year-old hearts pump blood as well as those of typical 40 year olds. "While many important physiologic variables show substantial losses with advancing age on the average, an important characteristic of such age-grouped data is the substantial variability within groups," two researchers, John W. Rowe, former director of the National Institute on Aging, and Robert L. Kahn, of Harvard University, wrote in 1987. "In many data sets that show substantial average decline with age, one can find older persons with minimal physiologic loss, or none at all, when compared to the average of their younger counterparts." If one thinks of the older people he or she knows, it will be clear that their physical and mental abilities vary greatly.

Another reason for hope is that although some of the deterioration that comes with age is inevitable, much is not. Just how much is inevitable is not known, but the contribution of life-style—diet, exercise, and other things that can be controlled—to the aging process is believed to be significant. This belief represents a major change of attitude. Until fairly recently, the physical deterioration of age and the diseases that accompany it were regarded as inevitable consequences of the aging process, and medicine concentrated on treating them. Now the concentration is on prevention. There are two aspects of this preventive effort. One concentrates on life-style, singling out those harmful changes that are avoidable and working out the alterations in exercise, diet, and other controllable factors that can prevent them. One example is cardiac fitness: People who exercise regularly have hearts that pump blood better in old age than those who do not exercise.

The second part of the preventive effort looks at disease. Many of the degenerative changes of old age are now seen to be the results of specific illnesses and not as the inevitable results of aging. The change is most evident in thinking about the aging mind. The belief that old age brought a condition called *senility*, a weakening of the mind's powers caused by aging, no longer exists. It is now known that the healthy mind retains much of its capacity regardless of years. An unlucky minority of older people are afflicted with a condition called *dementia*, a word that covers a number of physical diseases that damage specific parts of the brain; the best known of them is Alzheimer's disease.

There is a similar feeling about the body—that many of the deteriorations that come with the passing years are caused by disease, not by aging in itself. So one focus of aging studies is an effort to distinguish between healthy aging and *pathology* (disease)—between the changes that everyone undergoes and those caused by disease conditions that can be prevented or treated.

One consequence of this new thinking is that aging is a matter of interest for young people. With luck, a teenager today will retain his or her body for six or seven or eight more decades. As Eubie Blake, the jazz pianist and composer, said as he approached his centenary, "If I knew I was going to live to be a hundred, I'd have taken better care of myself."

For young people today, that is no joke; it is excellent advice because aging is a continuous process, one that goes on steadily

This photo shows the jazz pianist Eubie Blake at age 95. He was born in 1885 in Baltimore, Maryland, the son of parents who had been slaves. Scientists do not fully understand what lets some people live longer than others, but a healthy life-style seems to help.

all through life. The human body does not hit a plateau at maturity, leveling off for years before the aging process begins. Instead, there is a linear process of aging that proceeds at a steady rate for decades. Someone who is 30 years old is aging at the same rate as someone who is 80. And so, youth is the time to begin preparing for old age.

In a paper written in 1987, Drs. Rowe and Kahn drew a distinction between two kinds of aging: "usual" aging, in which all the predicted changes in such things as heart function, blood pressure, and so on, occur as expected; and "successful" aging, in which the loss of physical and mental abilities and the onset of disease do not happen as predicted because they are prevented by diet, exercise, and other strategies.

Skin

To illustrate the possibility of preventive measures, the outermost part of the body, the skin, is a good example. There are striking changes in the skin with age. It becomes thinner and drier, heals more slowly, and becomes less able to do its part in protecting against the ill effects of temperature extremes. But the change that appears to bother people most is that older skin tends to be wrinkled.

Wrinkling and loss of elasticity are two of the effects of aging that have been regarded as inevitable. That has not made them any more bearable. One study found that women in their thirties and forties thought that the worst thing about growing old was wrinkles. However, women aged 65 had stopped worrying about them. Today *dermatologists* (doctors specializing in the skin) regard the wrinkles of old age as largely avoidable if one simple measure is taken: avoidance of prolonged exposure to sunlight's damaging *ultraviolet radiation*—radiation with a wavelength between those of visible light and X rays. Curiously, that is a point that has to be stressed most with young people.

A lot of people still think of sunlight as beneficial and consider a tan to be a sign of health. That view is left over from bygone years when slum children who were poorly housed and fed could develop *rickets*, a disease characterized by soft or deformed bones, because they never saw sunlight. Sunlight converts a chemical in the body to vitamin D, which is essential for sound bones. Today, rickets is rare, but damage from overexposure to sunlight is common. Dermatologists now believe that skin will look younger longer if people avoid exposure to the damaging radiation in sunlight by staying out of the sun or by using adequate amounts of sunscreen preparations that block ultraviolet radiation. Those measures also help prevent skin cancer. There is evidence that precancerous skin changes can be reversed by use of a prescription lotion containing resorcinol, sold under the brand name Retin-A, first developed as an acne medication. Evidence that resorcinol can slow the aging of skin is still lacking at this writing, however.

This advice about aging skin should be taken to heart by young people because most of the solar damage that causes premature wrinkling is believed to occur before age 20. Teenagers who protect themselves from damaging sunlight will look better 20, 30, and 40 years down the road. Dermatologists, who are concerned more about the rising incidence of skin cancer than about wrinkles, are conducting a major campaign to make the "pale look" as socially acceptable as a tan is now. It is hard to tell whether they will succeed, but it can be predicted that teenagers who follow their advice will have better skin when they are old than those who do not.

The Cardiovascular System and the Respiratory System

What is true of the skin is also true of the *cardiovascular system*, the heart and the blood vessels. It is especially important to separate the effects of disease from normal aging because cardiovascular diseases, such as heart attack and stroke, are the leading causes of death in the United States, responsible for half the deaths in people over 65. The incidence of coronary disease increases dramatically with age, affecting two-thirds of all men in their seventies and 60% of women in their eighties.

The Baltimore Longitudinal Study of Aging has studied individuals without coronary disease to see what happens as they grow older. A set of changes has been noted. *Systolic blood pressure*—the pressure when the heart contracts—rises moderately.

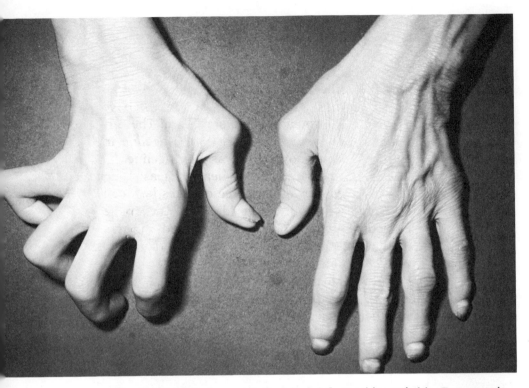

These hands have been crippled and deformed by arthritis. To some degree, arthritis affects most people as they age. It may cause only a slight stiffness in a few joints, but it also can be painfully incapacitating.

The *left ventricle*, the chamber of the heart that pumps blood to the body, grows slightly thicker, as does the *aorta*, the main *artery*, or blood vessel leading from the heart. The heart's pumping ability does not decline, but the rate at which it fills with blood after each contraction declines drastically.

Studies of *cardiac output*—the amount of blood pumped by the heart with each contraction—show the effects of disease. One test done for the Longitudinal Study of Aging found a striking decrease in cardiac output with age, during exercise, in a randomly selected group of 233 volunteers, none of whom appeared to have heart disease. But when careful studies were done of health function, many of these apparently healthy individuals were found to have "silent" heart disease. Those were the ones whose heart was pumping less blood. People with healthy hearts had no reduction in cardiac output.

The same is true of the *respiratory system*, which brings oxygen into the body and eliminates carbon dioxide as a waste product. The maximum amount of oxygen that the lungs can expel is regarded as a major indicator of physical fitness. Several studies have shown that lung function will decline to about 75% of its peak value by age 80 in nonsmokers. Cigarette smokers will have only 40% of their peak lung function at the same age. There is some evidence that regular exercise can reduce the decline in lung function as well as help to slow cardiovascular decline.

The history of *cardiovascular disease*—heart disease and stroke—in the United States during the three decades between 1960 and 1990 is a major triumph of the idea that preventive measures can keep people young longer. In that period, the age-adjusted heart attack death rate declined by 40% and the death rate from stroke by 50%. Rates are adjusted for age because they increase with age. Most Americans still die of cardiovascular disease, but later than they did before—in their seventies or eighties rather than their forties or fifties.

Those reductions are attributed to better health habits—less cigarette smoking, diets lower in fat, more exercise, detection and treatment of high blood pressure—the latter being the most important factor in preventing stroke.

The Musculoskeletal System

The *musculoskeletal system*—the bones and muscles—also has its normal changes and its diseases of age. One disease, *osteoporosis*, the thinning of bones, affects mostly women. Arthritis affects almost everyone. There are two kinds of arthritis. *Rheumatoid arthritis*, which can occur at any age, results in destruction of the joints and is believed to be caused by an immune defect. The more common kind, *osteoarthritis*, is the one older people suffer from. It is primarily caused by wear and tear, the cumulative damage done by decades of use. One of the bad things that can be said about exercise is that it can lead to osteoarthritis, which often afflicts professional athletes. Sandy Koufax, the Hall of Fame pitcher, quit at the height of his career because of the damage done by osteoarthritis to his pitching arm.

Muscle also changes with age. In general, there is a loss of muscle mass, which is replaced by fat. In addition, muscles become less flexible, as do their supporting tendons and *ligaments*

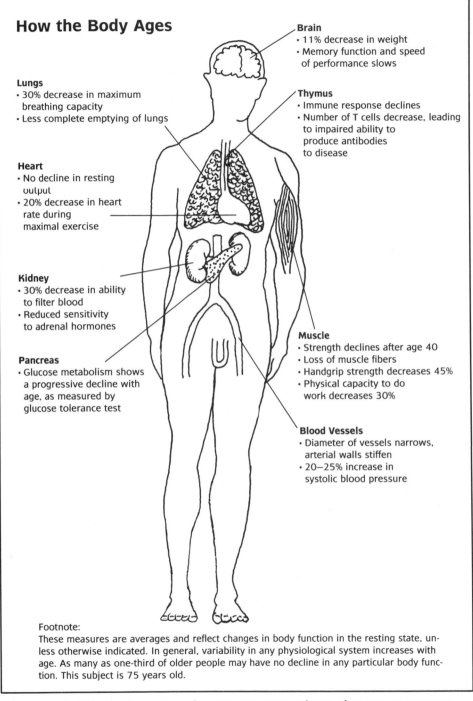

How the Body Ages

Brain
- 11% decrease in weight
- Memory function and speed of performance slows

Lungs
- 30% decrease in maximum breathing capacity
- Less complete emptying of lungs

Thymus
- Immune response declines
- Number of T cells decrease, leading to impaired ability to produce antibodies to disease

Heart
- No decline in resting output
- 20% decrease in heart rate during maximal exercise

Kidney
- 30% decrease in ability to filter blood
- Reduced sensitivity to adrenal hormones

Pancreas
- Glucose metabolism shows a progressive decline with age, as measured by glucose tolerance test

Muscle
- Strength declines after age 40
- Loss of muscle fibers
- Handgrip strength decreases 45%
- Physical capacity to do work decreases 30%

Blood Vessels
- Diameter of vessels narrows, arterial walls stiffen
- 20–25% increase in systolic blood pressure

Footnote:
These measures are averages and reflect changes in body function in the resting state, unless otherwise indicated. In general, variability in any physiological system increases with age. As many as one-third of older people may have no decline in any particular body function. This subject is 75 years old.

All of the body parts and organ systems undergo changes as a person ages. The extent of these changes may vary from person to person, but the general patterns are the same for all people.

(connective tissue that links bone to bone), so that injuries occur more often and take longer to heal. This can be seen by observing professional ballplayers early in life. Athletes in their twenties heal faster than those in their thirties and forties. For all athletes, whether in their thirties or in their seventies, the recommendation for avoiding injury is the same: Warm up adequately, giving muscles and ligaments time to stretch.

The Digestive System

The *digestive system*, including the esophagus, stomach, large and small intestines, and other digestive organs, also works a little less efficiently with age. Food moves through the digestive tract more slowly, and the ability to absorb some nutrients is reduced. The incidence of digestive disorders also increases. All these changes make a balanced diet more important for older people than for the young.

CANCER

One of the most prominent features of aging is that the incidence of cancer increases. The increase is true for virtually all kinds of cancer in both sexes. The reason for the increase is not known, but it seems obvious that some of the body's protective mechanisms become less efficient with age. Whether the problem is caused by a decline in immune defenses, an increased rate of mutations in genetic material, a combination of the two, or other factors is unclear, but the relationship between increased age and increased incidence of cancer is undeniable.

The focus these days is not on the inevitability of cancer but on its prevention by changes in life-style. These changes are a matter for young people to think about because cancer generally takes many years to develop. The clearest preventive message is about the most common form of cancer. Most cases of lung cancer, probably at least 80% of them, could be prevented if people did not smoke cigarettes. This is a message for young people because it takes 20 or more years of cigarette smoking to induce lung cancer. There is good evidence that cancers of the digestive tract can be prevented by diets that are lower in fat and higher in fiber and vitamin-rich vegetables than most Americans now eat. The same kind of diet is believed to help prevent breast cancer. Skin cancer, including the deadly form called *malignant melanoma*, can be prevented by minimizing exposure to the ultraviolet radiation in sunlight.

So although some parts of the aging process are bound to affect everyone, many can be minimized or avoided through preventive measures. Following basic advice on health throughout the years—eating a balanced diet, exercising, and avoiding cigarettes and prolonged, unprotected sun exposure—can help a person enjoy a long, healthy life.

•   •   •   •

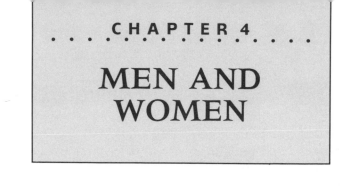

CHAPTER 4

MEN AND WOMEN

Everyone ages, but men and women age differently. One important difference is that women outlive men in developed countries such as the United States. On the average, an American woman will live seven years longer than an American man. This was not always so. Until the 20th century, men tended to outlive women because of the high toll taken by childbearing. American women now have fewer babies than they did a century ago. They also have much better medical care during pregnancy and when they deliver their babies. As a result, death in childbearing is now uncommon, and old women outnumber old men.

Why do women live longer than men? The National Institute on Aging estimates that two-thirds of the difference in survival can be explained by life-style. Women smoke less, take better care of themselves, and engage in dangerous jobs and activities less frequently. The remaining one-third of the difference in survival appears to be a matter of basic biology; women seem to be built to last longer than men. This difference starts even before birth. About 170 males are conceived for every 100 females. The *wastage rate*, those lost through miscarriage, is higher for male embryos than females; 105 boys are born for every 100 girls. Male *attrition*, reduction in number, continues through youth, so that the number of boys and girls is equal at adolescence. Women continue to gain steadily after that. The reasons are not clear, but nature does seem to have designed women more sturdily than men.

In developed countries, women tend to live longer than men, in part because they take better care of themselves and are exposed to fewer risks throughout life but also because of biological differences.

MENOPAUSE

The most obvious age-related change that differentiates women from men is menopause. Women experience it; men do not. Menopause is defined as the end of menstruation plus one year. Its underlying cause is a sharp reduction in the production of estrogen, the female sex hormone. There has long been speculation about the existence of male menopause. Current belief is that there is no such thing. That belief is based on a large number of studies showing that there is no sudden, sharp decrease in production of *testosterone*, the male sex hormone, comparable to what happens with estrogen. And whereas women cannot have babies after menopause, most men remain fertile into their seventies and even beyond.

Menopause does not occur all that suddenly. In most women, the time leading up to menopause, called the *climacteric*, can last a year. Menstrual periods generally become irregular before they end; some women experience heavier bleeding than usual at times during the climacteric. The average age of menopause in the United States is 50 (compared to 46 in 1900), but it can occur at any point from the late thirties to the late fifties. Because the average female life span is 70-odd years, most American women will now spend a third or more of their life in the post-menopausal years.

Some women experience menopause simply as the cessation of menstrual periods. Others experience symptoms that can be troubling. There may be mood swings, tension, irritability, and crying spells. But depression and many physical problems often attributed to menopause are believed to be a general result of the aging process and are experienced by men as well as women.

One condition associated with menopause is *hot flashes*, experienced by three-quarters of women. There is a surge of heat to the chest, neck, face, and arms, accompanied by reddening of the skin, a faster pulse, and shallow breathing. A hot flash lasts no longer than a few minutes and is often followed by a chilled feeling and breathlessness. Hot flashes are generally not incapacitating, but about 1 woman in 10 finds them disturbing enough to seek medical treatment.

The conventional treatment is *estrogen replacement therapy*, the use of estrogen supplements to replace the hormones that the body no longer produces after menopause. Estrogen supplements can reduce hot flashes and relieve other menopausal symptoms, but they are the subject of some controversy. Estrogen therapy was introduced in the 1960s as a way to stay "forever feminine." It came under fire, as critics charged that the male-dominated medical establishment was defining a natural phenomenon as a pathological disease state requiring medical treatment, but the therapy still became widespread.

The potential dangers of estrogen supplements became evident in the 1970s when studies showed a threefold or higher incidence of cancer of the *endometrium*, the lining of the uterus, in postmenopausal women receiving estrogen replacement therapy. More recently, questions have been raised about a link between estrogen replacement therapy and breast cancer. A Swedish study in 1989 found such a link, with a higher incidence of breast cancer in women who took estrogen for prolonged periods. The study was not regarded as conclusive, however, because the number of women in the study was small and because the Swedish women took a form of estrogen not widely used in the United States.

Nevertheless, estrogen replacement therapy is still widely used, although with many precautions, in cases where its benefits are believed to outweigh its hazards. Those benefits are believed to apply not only to hot flashes but also to osteoporosis, another condition closely associated with menopause.

OSTEOPOROSIS

Osteoporosis is a gradual thinning of the bones that afflicts far more women than men and usually occurs after menopause. About 30% of women eventually will have some degree of osteoporosis. It most often affects the bones of the spine, hip, wrists, and legs. Bones can become so thin they break spontaneously; complications of hip fractures are a leading cause of death in older women.

Estrogen replacement therapy can reduce osteoporosis. But hormone treatment clearly is not the whole story regarding osteoporosis. Many preventive measures for women do not involve estrogen. The most effective preventive measures appear to be

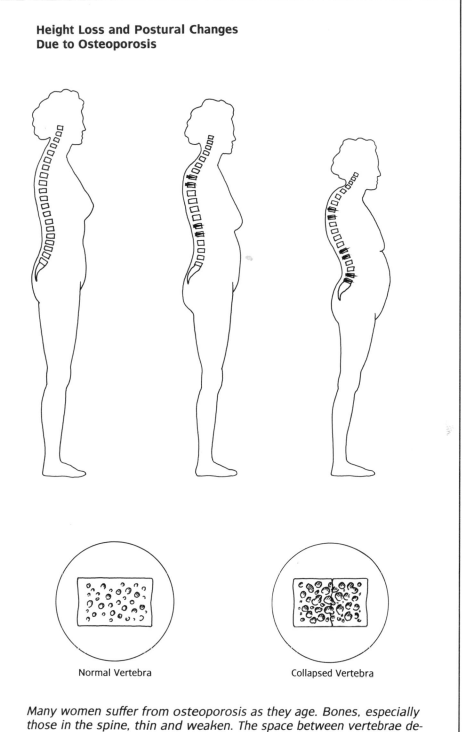

**Height Loss and Postural Changes
Due to Osteoporosis**

Normal Vertebra

Collapsed Vertebra

Many women suffer from osteoporosis as they age. Bones, especially those in the spine, thin and weaken. The space between vertebrae decreases, and the vertebrae thin, causing curvature.

those that are started well before menopause, especially for those women identified as being at highest risk: fair-skinned, delicately built Caucasians. For unknown reasons, black women are less vulnerable to osteoporosis than are white women.

The best way to prevent osteoporosis is to build bone mass before menopause. It is best to start young, during the teen years, because bone mass reaches its peak at about age 35. A good intake of *calcium*, a crucial ingredient of bone, is strongly recommended. The preferable method is to eat foods rich in calcium, such as milk and other dairy products, but it is also wise to avoid foods that interfere with bone metabolism: soda pop, red meat, and coffee among them. The recommended intake for women is 1 gram of calcium a day before menopause and 1.5 grams a day after menopause. Most American women get far less; one study found that 75% of women over the age of 35 got less than 800 milligrams (four-fifths of a gram) of calcium daily. The role of calcium supplements is somewhat controversial. Most experts prefer calcium from dietary sources. If calcium supplements are taken, it should be relatively early in life because there is no clear evidence of their benefit after menopause.

Another reason that estrogen replacement therapy is controversial is that it must be continued for many years to be effective against osteoporosis, and the risk of endometrial cancer is related to the length of use. But fortunately, the form of endometrial cancer related to estrogen supplements can be detected early and treated effectively. The addition of another hormone, *progestogen*, to the therapy greatly reduces the risk of endometrial cancer, although the 1989 Swedish study found that the addition of progestogen might increase the risk of breast cancer.

The issue is still being studied, but a consensus meeting of experts at the National Institutes of Health in 1987 gave cautious approval to estrogen replacement therapy, with careful monitoring of women taking it, on the grounds that the benefits outweighed the adverse effects. Among other things, the experts noted that replacement therapy has beneficial effects for the female genital tract. But the experts also said that a decision to give estrogen replacement therapy must be based on each woman's unique needs. And it should not be given to women with coronary artery disease; high blood pressure; circulatory problems; liver, kidney, or bladder disease; diabetes; or asthma.

PROSTATE PROBLEMS

A major problem for older men that women do not have is *prostate* trouble. The prostate is a small gland that surrounds the *urethra*, the tube that carries urine from the bladder. It produces fluid necessary for sperm transport. Women do not have a prostate gland. For unknown reasons, the prostate begins to enlarge with age. About 80% of men over the age of 50 experience this condition, which is called *benign prostatic hypertrophy* and makes urination more difficult or more frequent. If the problem is annoying enough, surgery may be performed to remove some prostate tissue.

The prostate is also vulnerable to infection, which can cause it to become inflamed. Infection can be treated by antibiotics and, if necessary, surgery. A more serious problem is prostate cancer, the incidence of which increases with age. It is the second most common cancer in men, after lung cancer. Regular examinations are recommended for all men over the age of 50 to detect prostate cancer. Detected early, it can often be cured. If it goes unnoticed, it can spread and become life threatening. Surgical removal of the prostate is the standard measure if cancer is found. In the past, that surgery has meant *impotence*, the inability to have or to maintain an erection long enough to have sexual intercourse. New surgical techniques now make it possible to preserve potency in many cases.

INCONTINENCE

An embarrassing condition that affects older women more than men is urinary incontinence. Men are vulnerable to this condition; one of every six older men suffers from it. But incontinence is more common in women, partly because childbearing weakens the pelvic muscles that control urinary flow. In addition, infections of the urinary tract become more common after menopause; their symptoms can include more frequent urination and loss of small amounts of urine with movements that put pressure on the bladder—even something as simple as a laugh.

The same phenomenon can happen without an infection. It is called stress incontinence. Another form, urge incontinence, is a release of urine without warning. A number of techniques can reduce or eliminate incontinence. They include exercises in which the pelvic muscles are tightened and relaxed repetitively, thus increasing their strength. In some cases, surgery can correct the problem. Behavior therapy and biofeedback have been effective in some studies. A major effort is being put into research on incontinence not only because of the human aspects of the condition but also for financial reasons. Incontinence is one of the major reasons for admission of older people to nursing homes.

Incontinence is one subject that was once unmentionable but is now out in the open. Sex and the older person is another such subject. There once was an unspoken assumption that sexual desire and performance disappeared with the passing years. In some cases, that is true—more true for men than for women.

IMPOTENCE

Impotence—technically, the inability to perform in 25% or more of sexual encounters—affects an increasing number of men as they age. Although fewer than 5% of men under the age of 45 are impotent, more than half the men over 75 are. But that leaves a large percentage of men who can function sexually even at that age.

Impotence was once thought to always have psychological rather than physical causes. More recent studies show that it often has a physical origin. Illness is a major cause of impotence. Prostate surgery is one possible cause. Diabetes can be another. Some medications interfere with sexual performance, as does overuse of alcohol or other recreational drugs. Many men who have had heart attacks are fearful of having sex, although those fears are usually unfounded and can be overcome by counseling.

Older men experience physical changes that affect sexual performance. It may take longer to attain an erection, and the erection may not be as firm or as large as in the younger years. The time needed to achieve another erection can be longer. But if the desire is there—as it is in a large percentage of men—a satisfactory sex life is still possible.

OTHER SEXUAL PROBLEMS

Women experience their own physical changes, most of them related to the reduction of estrogen production that comes with

Although many older men may have a problem with impotence, not all of them do. Doctors have developed ways of preventing or curing impotence. Many older couples continue to have and enjoy sexual intercourse.

menopause. Vaginal tissues become drier, so that pain and irritation can occur during intercourse. The vagina may become shorter and narrower, making intercourse difficult. Its walls become thinner, and vaginal secretions become less acidic, both factors that increase the possibility of vaginal infections. As mentioned, estrogen replacement therapy can slow or prevent many of these changes, making sexual activity more enjoyable.

A *hysterectomy*, surgical removal of the uterus, done for medical reasons or as a type of sterilization, can affect sexuality for physical or psychological reasons. If the surgeon removes too much of the uterus, sexual performance may become difficult or impossible. In other cases, the psychological impact of hysterectomy can be so great that a woman gives up sex. Counseling can help in such cases.

Many of the psychological problems that formerly interfered with sexual performance in the later years, for men and women alike, have been eased because of increased acceptance of sexuality in older people. There is less talk of "dirty old men" these days. Sex is accepted as an integral part of older life, although its role is somewhat different than it is for the young.

"Sex in later life has more to do with intimacy than with the actual act of sex," says Myrna Lewis of the National Institute on Aging. "Many people tell us that, for them, sex is the opportunity to express admiration, loyalty and affection for another person. One older couple described their sex life as a port in the storm. Others describe a renewed sense of romance, a general affirmation of life, a special expression of joy and a continuing opportunity for growth."

•   •   •   •

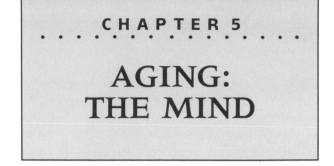
AGING:
THE MIND

Although the terms *mind* and *brain* are often used to refer to the same thing, there is an important distinction. The brain is the physical organ in which thoughts, emotions, and perceptions occur. *Mind* refers to the thoughts, emotions, and perceptions that a person experiences. The brain ages, like any physical organ, but how the mind changes with age is a complex question.

Ideas about the mind and the aging process have been clarified remarkably during the 1970s and 1980s. The idea that there is something called senility that weakens mental powers as one ages has been abandoned completely; it is now relegated to the attic with other medical antiques. Another idea that has been abandoned is the belief that mental function inevitably declines with age because nerve cells in the brain die and are not replaced.

This is not true. The mind, like the body, does change with age, and in parallel ways. Some kinds of memory can work more slowly, and some intellectual functions can be less efficient. But these forms of decline are often inconsequential for people who remain healthy. And they can be counterbalanced by improvement in the use of accumulated knowledge and information to make judgments and solve problems; in other words, wisdom.

The real cause of the majority of problems that affect mental function in old people is not aging itself but disease. The death of brain cells that is supposed to weaken the mind is in fact unimportant. Recent studies have shown that the critical factor in mental function is not the number of brain cells but the number of connections between brain cells. Intellectual stimulation causes nerve cells in the brain to grow more *dendrites*, extensions that make contact with other nerve cells. Studies show that brain cells do not lose their ability to make new connections with age. The active old brain can respond to stimuli in the environment as efficiently as the active young brain.

DEPRESSION AND INSOMNIA

The older brain, like the older body, is more vulnerable to damage and disease. But as with the body, it is a difference in degree and not in kind. The mental problems encountered in old age can be seen in younger people; they are simply more common in the old. And that is not true of all maladies. Until recently, depression was assumed to be more common in older people than in younger people because of losses suffered with the years. Clinical depression is a true disease, caused by a chemical imbalance in the brain, but it can be triggered by life events. But according to Dr. Benjamin Liptzin of the Harvard Geriatric Education Center, "Careful analysis, including large-scale epidemiologic studies in the community, suggests that clinical depression is less common in the elderly than it is among people under age 75." Whereas 10% of people over 65 have significant symptoms of depression, only 2% have clinical depression requiring aggressive treatment, Dr. Liptzin estimates. And the Baltimore Longitudinal Study of Aging has found that older people can cope with stress as well

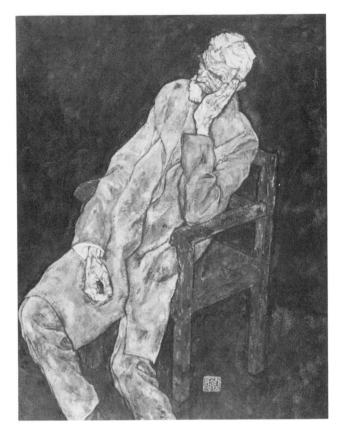

Portrait of an Old Man
*(1916) by Egon Schiele.
Until recently it was as-
sumed, wrongly, that the
elderly suffer from
depression more than
the young.*

as young people can. Faced with a death in the family, illness, or other stresses, old people react in much the same way as the young, the study finds.

One problem that does appear to be more common in older people is difficulty in sleeping. In a 1988 Gallup Poll, 40% of people over 60 said they experienced some kind of sleep problem. In general, older people sleep less than when they were young—not because they need less sleep but because they are more sensitive to noises and lights and so are more easily aroused. In addition, many illnesses that are common in older people can interfere with sleep, as can some prescription drugs and over-the-counter medications.

Insomnia in the old is treated the same way as in younger people, with therapy that stresses the learning of good sleep habits: going to bed and getting up at regular times, avoiding daytime

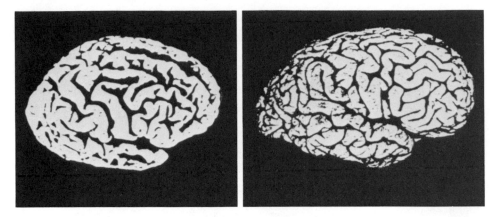

The brain on the right is a normal, healthy brain. The brain on the left has been affected by Alzheimer's disease, which contributes to the widening of valleys, or sulci, on the brain's surface.

naps, getting adequate exercise, avoiding undue stimulation at bedtime. Sleep medications are reserved for short-term use in limited situations because of the risk of addiction and other adverse side effects. If depression is the problem that causes sleep disturbances—most people with depression have trouble sleeping—insomnia is approached by treating depression with antidepressant drugs, with psychotherapy, or both. In most cases, depression is treatable.

ALZHEIMER'S DISEASE

A serious and not very treatable condition that is tragically common in the elderly is Alzheimer's disease, a degenerative disease of the brain that has emerged as one of the nation's major health problems. Alzheimer's disease can strike people in their forties, but its incidence goes up sharply with age. In all, 6% of Americans aged 65 or older have Alzheimer's disease, but the incidence rises to 40%—2 of every 5 people—over the age of 85. Between 2.5 million and 3 million Americans now have it, and the number will rise as the elderly population grows.

Alzheimer's disease was described almost a century ago by Alois Alzheimer, the German doctor for whom it was named, but it has been recognized as a major problem only in the past two decades. In one respect, that recognition is a major advance because a recognized disease is easier to deal with than the ill-defined concept of senility. The accepted medical term now is *senile dementia*, which describes Alzheimer's and other degenerative diseases.

Alzheimer's disease is mostly a mystery. Its cause is unknown, and it is even difficult to diagnose correctly. It usually has a gradual, insidious onset. People begin to have trouble remembering recent events and performing familiar tasks. They often become confused. They may have trouble finding words and finishing thoughts. Personality traits and behavior can change; a tranquil person can suddenly become violent. As the disease progresses, patients become less and less functional, until they need constant care.

Researchers can describe physical changes in the brain of Alzheimer's disease patients. In autopsies, they see *plaques*, which are clusters of degenerating nerve cell endings, and *tangles*, masses of twisted filaments that accumulate in nerve cells. There is an accumulation of *amyloid*, a starchy substance that contains

The presence in the brain of both plaques (left), or clusters of degenerating nerve cell endings, and tangles (right), or masses of twisted nerve cell filaments, is characteristic of Alzheimer's disease.

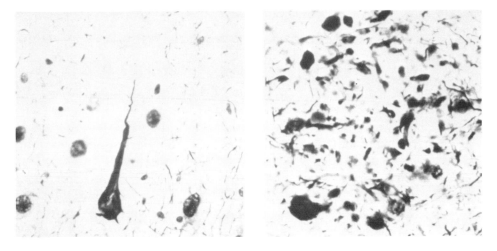

protein fragments. Studies of brain chemistry find abnormally low levels of *acetylcholine*, a chemical that transmits signals between nerve cells, in the areas where the plaques, tangles, and amyloid are found.

At this time, there is no explanation to tie these findings together or suggest what causes the brain cell abnormalities. Inheritance is believed to play a role, but that role is not clear. In 1987, Peter St. George-Hyslop and other researchers at Massachusetts General Hospital in Boston reported detection of a specific genetic defect in a form of Alzheimer's disease that runs in families and strikes relatively early in life. The report caused great excitement because it appeared to open a door to a full understanding of Alzheimer's disease by bringing together a number of different clues.

The genetic defect related to Alzheimer's disease was on chromosome 21 (all human genes are collected in bodies called chromosomes, which have been numbered). A genetic defect involved in *Down's syndrome*—a genetic disease that causes mental retardation—has also been found on chromosome 21. The two conditions appear to be related: In addition to causing mental retardation, Down's syndrome also causes progressive deterioration of the kind observed in Alzheimer's disease. The gene for amyloid has also been reported to be on chromosome 21.

The solution has since unraveled. Other researchers who studied other patients with the familial form of Alzheimer's disease did not find the chromosome 21 defect that the Boston group reported. The thought that the defect was in the amyloid gene has proved to be unfounded; the exact role of amyloid in Alzheimer's disease is not clear. More research is being done on the genetics of Alzheimer's disease.

Another thought is that a *virus*, an acellular parasite, is implicated in Alzheimer's disease. In 1989, Dr. Elias Manuelidis and others at Yale University found that hamsters that were injected with blood cells from relatives of Alzheimer's patients suffered brain damage. The implication is that the damage was done by a virus in the blood cells. Another, much more rare degenerative brain disease called *Creutzfeldt-Jakob disease* is known to be caused by a slow virus, one that causes a degenerative disease that develops slowly long after infection by the virus. No virus has been found in Alzheimer's patients as yet, but the search goes on.

At this writing, the best-educated guess is that Alzheimer's disease is caused by a combination of genetic and environmental factors. Aluminum is under suspicion as one of those factors, because high levels of aluminum have been found in Alzheimer's plaques. But aluminum is widespread in nature, and no definite connection has been made between it and Alzheimer's disease.

While the search for a cause goes on, so does the search for a treatment. At this writing, only one drug has been approved for treatment of Alzheimer's disease—*ergot alkaloid*, a relative of drugs used for migraine headaches. It appears to improve the functioning of patients but does not stop progression of the disease. Several strategies are being tried to develop more effective treatments. One is the use of medications that increase the brain's supply of acetylcholine. Another employs a newly discovered natural substance, *nerve growth factor*, to prevent the death of brain cells. Nerve growth factor is normally produced in small amounts by the body. Its gene has been isolated and cloned, making mass production possible through genetic engineering. At this writing, nerve growth factor is one of several drugs being tested in patients.

OTHER DEGENERATIVE BRAIN CONDITIONS

Alzheimer's disease is not the only cause of senile dementia. About 1 case in 12 is due to a condition called *multi-infarct dementia*, which is the result of a number of tiny strokes that progressively kill brain cells. It is found in people with a history of high blood pressure, blood vessel disease, or a previous stroke. Multi-infarct dementia is the medical term for what is commonly but inaccurately known as hardening of the arteries of the brain. Severe depression can cause the same symptoms, as can a deficiency of vitamin B_{12}. A variety of relatively rare conditions are responsible for about 1 case in 10 of senile dementia. It is often difficult for doctors to tell what is causing the problem. A major research effort is being made to develop a specific diagnostic test for Alzheimer's disease so that it can be distinguished from other causes of senile dementia that require different treatments.

(continued on page 66)

Faces of the Elderly
Around the World

The faces of those who have seen many years come and go show a uniqueness that only develops with age. The lines on a person's face are as individual as a fingerprint. They grow out of decades of joys and sorrows. These faces are etched by life itself.

Woman from Fayum, Egypt

Unidentified man

Woman from the Banjara
tribal community near
Hyderabad, India

Man from Djakarta, Indonesia

Unidentified woman

Man from Morocco

Unidentified women

Woman from Japan

Seminole Indian woman

Man from Columbus, Ohio

Man from Tehran, Iran

Man from Bukhara, USSR

Laotian refugee of the Hmong tribe

Man from Moscow, USSR

Unidentified man

Woman from the Banjara tribal
community near Hyderabad, India

Woman from Cairo, Egypt

Unidentified man

Unidentified man

Unidentified man

Unidentified man

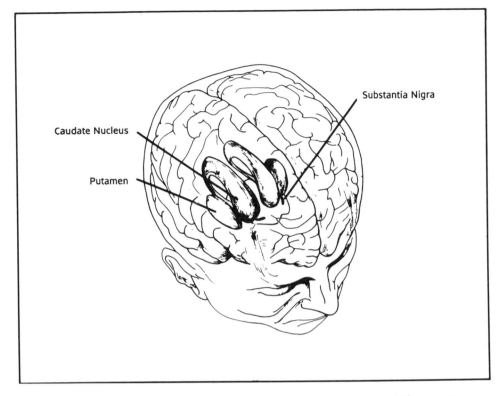

This diagram of the brain shows the caudate nucleus and the putamen, which together make up the basal ganglia, and the substantia nigra. A reduced amount of dopamine in the basal ganglia and the death of nerve cells in the substantia nigra lead to the symptoms of Parkinson's disease.

(continued from page 59)

Another degenerative brain condition whose effects can be almost as devastating as senile dementia is *Parkinson's disease.* Like Alzheimer's, Parkinson's can occur relatively early in life, as early as the thirties or forties, but it becomes much more common with age. Parkinson's disease causes muscle rigidity, slowness and stiffness of movement, and trembling, all of which become progressively more severe with time. These symptoms result from the death of nerve cells in a small part of the *brainstem* called the *substantia nigra* and from a depletion of the brain's supply of *dopamine*, another chemical that transmits signals between nerve cells. Dopamine is a signal transmitter for cells in the brain centers called *basal ganglia*, which are important in the control of body movements. The mainstay of treatment for Parkinson's disease is *L-dopa*, a compound that is taken orally and is converted to dopamine in the brain. L-dopa and all but one of the other drugs used to treat Parkinson's disease can reduce the severity of symptoms, but they do not stop the progression of the disease. The exception—a drug that apparently can stop the disease from getting worse—was found through one of the most remarkable biomedical detective stories of the century.

The story began in 1982 with faulty chemical work by an illicit laboratory in northern California that tried to manufacture a synthetic opiate, or opiumlike narcotic. The unknown chemists in this lab were trying to manufacture a street drug whose chemical name is *1-methyl-4-phenyl-4-proprionoxypiperidine*, abbreviated MPPP, which is a relative of heroin. Not long after MPPP appeared on the street, Dr. J. William Langston and other physicians at the Santa Clara Valley Medical Center began seeing young patients with all the symptoms of advanced Parkinson's disease. They traced the cause to the street drug—not MPPP itself but MPTP, a contaminated compound made accidentally during MPPP manufacture. Studies showed that MPTP destroys the cells of the substantia nigra, the brain center affected in Parkinson's disease.

Langston established the California Parkinson's Foundation and began working with other scientists to determine how MPPP is metabolized in the body and how its use results in the death of specific brain cells. Work by Neal Castagnali, Anthony Trever, and other chemists at the University of California, San Francisco, showed that the critical event is transformation of MPPP to MPTP by a brain chemical called *monoamine oxidase.*

Monoamine oxidase was already well known. It plays a role in depression; *monoamine oxidase inhibitors* are a widely used class of antidepressant drugs. The California researchers began testing a series of monoamine oxidase inhibitors on laboratory animals to see whether they could block the nerve damage inflicted by MPTP. They did. That work led to a trial in which *eldepryl,* a monoamine oxidase inhibitor approved for use in Parkinson's along with L-dopa, was given to patients to see whether it could prevent nerve damage in humans.

In August 1989, Dr. Langston and his colleagues reported that the first small trial, involving only 28 patients, showed that eldepryl slows the progression of Parkinson's disease, apparently by preventing the death of brain cells in the substantia nigra.

Eldepryl is the first drug that does more than just treat the symptoms of a degenerative brain disease. It also gives researchers a new insight into the underlying mechanisms of Parkinson's disease. There is a strong suspicion that many cases of Parkinson's disease are caused by some environmental toxin that acts in the same way as MPTP. Efforts to detect such a toxin are under way. In addition, the discovery could help find a common mechanism that causes the damage seen in Alzheimer's disease and other degenerative brain diseases.

•   •   •   •

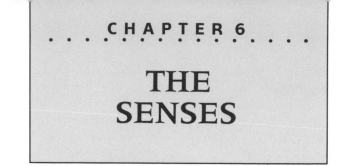

CHAPTER 6

THE SENSES

It is commonplace to talk about the aging sensory system in terms of loss. William Shakespeare calls old age the seventh age of man, describing it as "second childishness and mere oblivion, sans [without] teeth, sans eyes, sans taste, sans everything." And truly, it can happen that way. Older people are more likely to suffer loss of vision, hearing, taste, or smell. But sensory losses are not inevitable with age. There is good reason to believe they will be less common in the future, in part because Americans are generally healthier, in part because doctors know how to prevent them. And people who grow old now have the benefit of better ways to treat sensory problems when they occur.

TASTE

The sense of taste provides an example of how people now deal with aging. Like other sensory losses, a declining ability to taste is not exclusive to old age; it can happen to anyone at any time. Yet complaints about lack of taste are more common in older people. Conventional thought has attributed this decline to *atrophy*, or wasting away, of the taste buds, the minute organs on the tongue that detect different flavors. It has been assumed that the taste buds begin to atrophy after the age of 60. But researchers who have gone to the trouble of counting taste buds in older animals and humans have found no such loss. Explanations for a declining sense of taste in the elderly now center on diseases of the mouth, on dental health, and on oral hygiene.

Many older people wear dentures because they have lost many or all of their teeth. Ill-fitting dentures can interfere with the sense of taste. Poor oral hygiene—failure to brush and floss regularly—can also interfere with the sense of taste. So can an *oral abscess*, a pus-filled area in the mouth, which can result from infection or neglected dental decay. In addition, some medications can interfere with the sense of taste by reducing the flow of *saliva*, a secretion of the mouth that aids in digestion. So the sensory loss that many older people experience is something that can be managed by regular visits to the dentist and attention to tooth brushing, dentures, and medications.

Loss of ability to taste should be less of a problem for the coming generations of older Americans. Fewer Americans are losing their teeth because of *fluoridation* (the addition of stannous fluoride—a compound that helps prevent tooth decay—to the drinking water); better dental care; and improved measures to fight *periodontal disease*, which weakens the gums, bones, and other structures that support the teeth. Good oral hygiene in the early years of life will mean tastier meals decades later.

SMELL

The sense of smell is closely related to the sense of taste. If a person cannot smell a food, he or she will think it is tasteless. Loss of ability to taste and smell are often lumped together under the category of *chemosensory disorders*. An estimated 10 million Americans suffer from them, with disorders of the sense of smell more common than taste disorders.

Many people suffer a decline in the ability to smell as they get older. One study found major impairment in 60% of people over the age of 65; a quarter of the people with an impairment were classified as *anosmic*, meaning they had no sense of smell at all. In some cases, the loss is caused by nasal obstruction or allergies. But many times it is due to loss of olfactory nerve fibers, which carry smell messages to the brain, or to loss of the olfactory receptors that detect smells. Not much can be done medically to treat those olfactory losses.

HEARING

Hearing loss is widespread in older people; the estimate of the National Institute on Aging is that 25% of those over 65 and 90% of those 85 and over have some degree of *presbycusis*, the medical term for age-related hearing loss. Many of these kinds of hearing loss are treatable, if not preventable, but dealing with age-related hearing loss is made more difficult by the stigma it carries. For some reason, hearing loss is not too socially acceptable. Nobody takes it amiss if an older person wears eyeglasses, but a hearing aid is regarded as a social embarrassment, so that many older people who could benefit from such a device hesitate to wear one.

There are two kinds of hearing loss. Conduction hearing loss is caused by blockage of or damage to the mechanisms that transmit sound to the inner ear. People pick up sound with the *eardrum*, a membrane that sits an inch inside the *ear canal*. Its vibrations are transmitted by three linked bones—the *malleus*, *incus*, and *stapes*, collectively called the *ossicles*—to the *cochlea*, a fluid-filled spiral organ lined with fine hairlike nerve cells, ar-

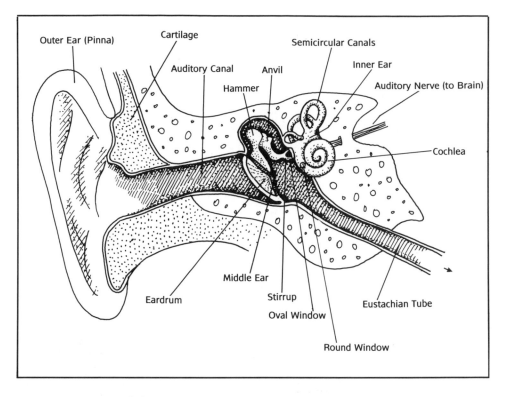

Diagram of the ear

ranged to pick up sounds of different frequencies. Signals from these nerve cells are transmitted to the brain via the auditory nerve.

Conduction hearing loss can be caused by something as simple as ear wax that blocks the ear canal leading to the eardrum. One reason why conduction hearing loss is more common in old age is that many older people do not clean their ears regularly. But the physical mechanism for sound transmission also becomes less efficient with age. The eardrum is not as flexible, the joints between the ossicles can harden, and a chronic ear infection can lead to scar formation. In addition, abnormal bone growth can cause deafness by immobilizing the stapes. This condition can be corrected by *stapedectomy*, a simple operation in which the bone is removed and replaced by a tiny wire. Most cases of conduction deafness can be treated successfully one way or another.

It is different with nerve deafness, which is caused by damage to the cochlea or the auditory nerve. A lot of this damage is preventable because it is caused by nothing but loud noise. Here is another instance where wisdom in the early years pays off later on. Popular music today is often loud—too loud for good hearing. A person can suffer permanent hearing loss by getting too close to the band at rock concerts or by turning up the volume on a portable stereo. And once the damage is done, it cannot be undone. The rule is: If the sound causes pain, it can cause hearing loss. Experts worry that loud rock music could be making the problem worse for people who will be old in the 21st century. A contributing factor is that American society is a very noisy one. The background noise in the streets, in trains and subways, and in the home is believed to contribute to a loss of high-frequency hearing ability that is common in older people.

Nerve hearing loss can also be caused by illness that cuts blood flow to the ear. Medications can also cause ear damage. Aspirin, for example, is linked to *tinnitus*, the ringing of the ears that irritates some people; some antibiotics can damage the auditory nerve. Older people are more vulnerable to these disorders because they take more medications.

Hearing aids can help people with either conduction or nerve deafness. Manufacturers are using microelectronics to make hearing aids smaller and less conspicuous, to overcome the common reluctance to be seen wearing one. But many older people with hearing loss do not take advantage of such devices because the problem is not recognized. Periodic hearing checkups, advisable at any age, are especially recommended in the later years.

SIGHT

Like the ear, the eye suffers ailments associated with age. Perhaps the most common is *presbyopia*, which is caused by the loss of flexibility that comes with passing years. Normally, the lens of the eye changes shape to focus on objects near and far. With age, the lens and the muscles that control it become less flexible, so focusing becomes more difficult. Presbyopia is the reason older people complain about not being able to read fine print. It is correctable with reading glasses or bifocals, which have separate lenses for distant seeing and close work.

An age-associated eye condition that is not so easily managed is *cataracts*, a gradual clouding of the lens. It is estimated that two-thirds of Americans aged 65 to 74 have some degree of lens clouding and that 15% eventually will require cataract surgery. Cataracts have a number of causes, centering on chemical changes in the proteins of the lens. Those changes are believed to be accelerated by exposure to the ultraviolet radiation in sunlight over many years. Sunglass lenses that block ultraviolet radiation are recommended for anyone who spends an appreciable amount of time in bright sunlight. That recommendation applies to young people because ultraviolet damage to the lens is cumulative, adding up over the years.

A more speculative way proposed to prevent cataract formation is to take antioxidants, such as vitamin C and E supplements.

These photos show how a person's vision is affected by cataracts, a gradual clouding of the lens, (left) and macular degeneration (right), a deterioration of the central portion of the retina.

A 1989 study by James McDonald Robertson and others at the University of Western Ontario in Canada found a 50% lower incidence of cataracts in older people who regularly took vitamin C and E supplements. The same group of researchers has done laboratory studies showing reduced symptoms of cataract formation in animals fed extra amounts of these vitamins. The rationale for the supplements is that vitamins C and E inactivate the free radicals that react with lens proteins to form cataracts. The evidence that antioxidants prevent cataracts is far from conclusive, however, and a large human study will probably be needed to prove that the method works.

Cataracts are treated by removing them surgically when they interfere too much with everyday living. Some people decide to wait longer than others. Cataract removal used to be major surgery, requiring a week of hospitalization. Today, most operations are done on an outpatient basis. A patient can go for the operation in the morning and be home by evening.

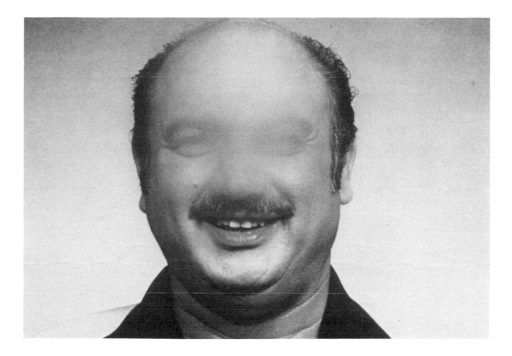

The usual technique is to make a small incision through which the lens is removed, an operation that can be done under local anesthesia. The lens is usually removed with a scalpel, but other techniques use enzymes or cryogenics, in which a chilled instrument adheres to the lens and then removes it. In most cases, removal is followed almost immediately by implantation of an artificial lens made of clear plastic. These intraocular lenses are not as good as the real thing, but they are much preferable to the thick "Coke bottle" eyeglasses that cataract patients once had to wear. Indeed, the combination of these intraocular lenses and special eyeglasses allows many cataract patients to have something close to normal vision. Soft contact lenses that can be worn for weeks or months at a time are an alternative. There can be complications, such as slippage of an intraocular lens, and some patients with other eye problems still require hospitalization, but generally cataract surgery is much less troublesome than it was 20 years ago.

The situation is less bright for *macular degeneration*, another eye condition that can cause blindness and is common in older people. It occurs in 11% of people aged 65 to 75 and in 30% of those over 75. Macular degeneration is deterioration of the *macula*, the central portion of the *retina*, which is responsible for sharp-focus vision and people's ability to distinguish colors. Its cause is unknown, and the degeneration cannot be stopped in most cases. Treatment with laser beams—beams of electromagnetic radiation—can help in the 10% of cases where leaky blood vessels in the retina are the cause of obstructed vision. The laser beams seal off the leaky vessels, preventing further bleeding.

Unlike macular degeneration, *glaucoma*, another common cause of vision loss in the elderly, is preventable. The problem in glaucoma is faulty drainage of fluid from the eye. In the most prevalent form of the disease, pressure builds up slowly and painlessly until it begins to destroy the optic nerve. A relatively rare form of glaucoma causes a sudden, painful buildup that requires emergency treatment. Glaucoma can be detected by a simple pressure test that adds only a few seconds to any eye examination. Once detected, it usually can be held in check by a daily application of eye drops. If eye drops do not work, laser beams can be used to burn tiny holes that open drainage for eye fluid.

Glaucoma blinds about 8,000 Americans each year. Diabetes blinds another 4,700 because it affects blood vessels in the retina. The condition called *diabetic retinopathy* weakens the veins of the retina. They swell and break, damaging the sensitive tissue. An overgrowth of blood vessels causes further damage. Good control of blood sugar levels can help keep diabetic retinopathy in check. Laser treatments can limit damage by sealing off leaky blood vessels.

Whereas these conditions can cause total blindness, a larger problem in terms of numbers of people affected is low vision, enough loss of visual function to interfere seriously with essential

Many older people who do not have degenerative eye disease still have problems with their vision. This woman both wears glasses and uses a magnifying glass to read the newspaper.

tasks. A 1977 U.S. government health survey estimated that there are 400,000 Americans who are legally blind and another 1 million with severe visual impairments, with 70% of the 1.4 million aged 65 or older. The number is expected to double by the year 2000 because there will be more older people then.

There are 250 low-vision clinics in the United States serving this population. They offer devices as simple as hand-held magnifying glasses and as complex as closed-circuit television systems that magnify reading matter. A listing of facilities offering low-vision services is maintained by the American Foundation for the Blind in New York City.

•　　　•　　　•　　　•

CHAPTER 7

NUTRITION

There are two ways to approach nutrition and aging. One is to look for a "magic formula," a set of foods or nutrients that can retard aging and prolong life. The other is to recommend a healthful but nonrevolutionary set of guidelines for sound nutrition. The first approach is more exciting and sells more books and magazines, but it is founded mostly on hope and speculation rather than scientific evidence. The second approach is the one taken by responsible experts on aging.

"MIRACLE" DIETS

The "miracle" diet approach is not new. It goes back at least to the 19th century, when Élie Metchnikoff, a bacteriologist who won the 1908 Nobel Prize in physiology or medicine, proposed that people who ate a lot of yogurt could prolong their life to the age of 150. His theory was based on his work with the *bacteria*, unicellular organisms lacking a distinct nuclear membrane, that inhabit the large intestine. Metchnikoff, who ate a lot of yogurt, died in 1916 at the age of 71.

Metchnikoff's theory and the many nutritional disappointments that have followed it have not deterred similar proposals. For the record, the prevailing opinion among those most knowledgeable about the scientific and medical evidence is that there is no diet that can prevent aging by interfering with the basic processes by which people grow old. The existence of this consensus does not stop the appearance of books that promote supposedly life-prolonging diets, however. There are always scraps of evidence gathered from scattered experiments that can be quoted in support of one proposed miracle diet or another.

These diets are usually based on one or another of the theories of aging discussed in Chapter 2. The most popular of them rely on high doses of specific substances, such as antioxidants (including vitamins E and C) or essential amino acids, that are supposed to prevent molecular reactions that cause aging. But as noted, decades of research have failed to produce conclusive proof for any of these theories, nor has work in the laboratory or with animals found any diet that prolongs life.

There is one exception, which was mentioned in Chapter 2. A diet that contains the bare minimum of calories and adequate amounts of nutrients can increase the life span of rats and mice by 50%. The rodents not only live longer but also avoid the diseases of old age longer. At this writing, the National Institute on Aging is testing the minimum diet on two species of monkeys. Results can be expected in the early 1990s. If the test produces positive results in the monkeys, people can then start asking themselves whether they want to eat a severely restricted diet all their life to put off old age and dying. It is too early to ask that question now.

Other miracle diets have no such evidence to back them up and can safely be ignored. However, it should be said that a large number of dietary recommendations can be made with some expectation that they can help prevent the major illnesses of old age, including cancer and heart disease. But these recommendations are made for people of all ages. What people eat when they are young can affect their well-being as they grow old.

HEALTHY DIETS

The basic prudent diet for graceful aging has been recommended in essentially identical form by many private and government agencies. It should have no more than 30% of its calories in the form of fat, rather than the 40% fat content of today's typical American diet. Most of the fat should be *unsaturated*, the kind found in vegetables and fish, rather than the *saturated* fats found in red meat and whole-milk dairy products. Protein should provide about 15% of caloric intake. The rest should be carbohy-

A healthy diet includes daily helpings of fruits and vegetables. Basically the same diet is recommended for the elderly as is recommended for the young.

drates, preferably the *complex carbohydrates* found in fruits, vegetables, and cereals rather than the *simple carbohydrates* found in table sugar. A diet with a good deal of complex carbohydrates will also provide substantial amounts of fiber, vitamins, and minerals. Evidence indicates that this prudent diet reduces the risk of heart disease and perhaps also of some forms of cancer if it is eaten throughout life.

In specific terms, a healthy diet includes the following foods daily.

- Two to five half-cup servings of vegetables, including dark green and yellow vegetables as well as potatoes and other starches
- One to four average-sized servings of fruits, preferably raw and whole, including one citrus fruit
- One to three cups of low-fat dairy products
- Three to six servings of whole-grain products (bread, rice, barley, corn, oatmeal, pasta)
- Three or more ounces of protein-rich foods such as chicken, meat, or fish
- Six to eight glasses of liquid each day, including two or three glasses of water

Although the basic prudent diet given above is recommended for people of all ages, some dietary recommendations do change with age. The last recommendation, for adequate liquid intake, is one nutritional need that does change somewhat with age. The American Dietetic Association says that as people age they need more water, noting that water "helps you to swallow food more easily. Water also aids digestion because you have less saliva and digestive fluid as you get older. Water also helps kidneys to function well."

There are two factors that alter nutritional requirements as people grow old. First, there is the set of changes that occur in the healthy body with age. Then there are the chronic diseases that are common in the elderly. A fair amount is known about the effect of disease on the nutritional status of older people. Hardly any research has been done on the changing nutritional needs of older people who do not have chronic diseases.

Geriatric Medicine by John Rowe and Richard Besdine, the standard textbook in the field, states, "Unfortunately, there has been little detailed scientific inquiry in this field. Of the approximately 50 nutrients that are essential in human nutrition, few have been specifically investigated as to their metabolism and requirements during advancing age in humans." Thus, the nutritional advice given to healthy older people is essentially the same as young people get, but with some exceptions.

Calcium

The recommendation for increased calcium intake in women after menopause is perhaps the most notable exception. As noted earlier, calcium is important in osteoporosis because it is the major structural element of bone. If there is not enough calcium in the diet, the body takes it out of bones, weakening them and leading to osteoporosis.

Researchers generally agree that calcium intake is important in the early years, when the body is growing and bone strength is established. The calcium intake recommended for women by a National Institutes of Health conference in 1987 is 1 gram (1,000 milligrams) a day. That level is about half the calcium intake measured in a U.S. Public Health Service survey of adult women. The dietary intake recommended for women past menopause who have other risk factors for osteoporosis is higher— 1,500 milligrams a day—because the body's ability to absorb calcium from food decreases with age. There is not much evidence that a high calcium intake after menopause can reverse osteoporosis. But as Dr. B. Lawrence Riggs of the Mayo Clinic said, "Until the final word is in, it would seem reasonable to err on the side of too much calcium rather than too little."

The aging body is less able to absorb not only calcium but other nutrients as well. Even in healthy older people, the intestinal tract becomes less efficient with the years. Another major physical change that happens in most people as they grow old is the replacement of lean muscle with fat. In a typical young adult, about 45% of body weight is muscle. In a typical 70 year old, muscle is about 25% of body weight. The lost muscle is replaced by fat. Older people who exercise vigorously, however, have a higher ratio of muscle to fat than the average.

Many other changes that could affect nutritional needs occur with age—starting with the molecules that are involved with the metabolism of food on the cellular level and ranging up to a general decline in the performance of most organ systems. Many older people suffer nutritional deficiencies because they lose their appetite for healthy food.

Good food just does not seem as appealing to someone who has suffered sensory loss or simply has reduced zest. The nutritional habits of older people can be adversely affected by reduced vision, decreased keenness of taste and smell, poor teeth, depression, and loneliness.

Vitamins and Minerals

The basic guidelines for nutrition are the Recommended Daily Allowances (RDAs) established by the Food and Nutrition Board of the National Academy of Sciences/National Research Council. The board sets RDAs for protein, 10 vitamins, and 6 minerals. An RDA is designed to be an adequate intake for the average healthy person. Published RDAs for adults are different for men and women, mostly because men weigh more on average, but they are identical for all adults after middle age. The same RDAs are recommended for all adults 51 years and older. "There is not a single nutrient for which there is a recommended daily allowance [specifically] for men and women 65 and older," says Dr. Myron Winick of Columbia University's Institute of Human Nutrition. "Even worse, there is no data base on which to formulate such recommendations."

It should also be noted that the RDAs are set to reach a negative goal: They are the minimum amounts required to avoid nutritional deficiency diseases. RDAs were first proposed decades ago, when vitamin and mineral deficiencies were real possibilities for a major portion of the American population. These days, a growing number of nutritionists believe that the RDAs should be adjusted to fit evidence that intake of certain nutrients can reduce the risk of illnesses. This proposal remains a minority view, yet it appears to be gaining influence. A major controversy erupted in 1986 when the Food and Nutrition Board proposed a reduction in the requirements for vitamins A and C, on the grounds that

An elderly woman in Miami, Florida, buys citrus fruit. Vitamin C, found in citrus, may help prevent certain forms of cancer and in one study has been shown to lower the incidence of cataracts.

the reduced amounts would still be enough to prevent nutritional deficiencies. There were counterproposals that the RDAs be increased because of some evidence that vitamins A and C may help prevent certain forms of cancer. In the end, the RDAs were left where they were.

Research may change that situation by giving new data on the effect of nutrients in specific conditions of old age. For example, in 1989 Dr. James McDonald Robertson, of the University of Western Ontario in Canada, reported on a study that compared 175 cataract patients with 175 people of the same age and background who had no cataracts. The only difference between the two groups was that the cataract-free people were more likely to have taken vitamin C and E dietary supplements in the previous five years. Those who took vitamin E supplements had a 50% lower incidence of cataracts; those who took vitamin C had a 70% reduction. Because the number of people in the study was small, Dr. Robertson suggested that "a randomized, controlled trial of vitamin supplementation in cataract prevention would be justified."

At the moment, most nutritional experts recommend that vitamin intake be maintained or increased by eating the appropriate foods, not by taking supplements. The reason is that most studies on nutrition and disease measure nutrient intake by looking at the foods people eat. That sort of study makes it difficult to say that a specific nutrient prevents a specific disease.

A good example was a study of diet and lung cancer done among Hawaiian men and women in the mid-1980s by a group of physicians at the University of Hawaii. They found a higher incidence of lung cancer in people who had the lowest intake of *beta-carotene*, a form of vitamin A. But the researchers also found that regular consumption of all vegetables was associated with a greater reduction of risk than that shown with vitamin A intake alone. "This observation suggests that other constituents of vegetables . . . may also protect against lung cancer in humans," they reported. The study concluded that more studies are needed to identify those constituents.

Alcohol and medications can also affect nutrition in the elderly. In small amounts—for example, a glass of wine in the evening—alcohol can help, by promoting relaxation and sharpening the appetite. In large amounts, alcohol can be devastating, especially for someone who is taking several medications, as many older people do.

Prescription and over-the-counter drugs can also contribute to nutritional deficiencies. Aspirin, often used for arthritis, can foster iron deficiency by causing bleeding in the stomach and intestine. Laxatives can interfere with the absorption of vitamin D. Many other drugs can also affect the nutritional status of an older person.

•   •   •   •

CHAPTER 8

MEDICINE AND THE ELDERLY

As the older population in the United States has increased, a new specialty has grown to meet new needs: geriatrics, the medicine of old age. The first institution to have a formal department of geriatrics was Mount Sinai Medical Center in New York, but most major medical centers now have sections devoted to the special needs of the elderly. Thus far there is no medical specialty of geriatrics comparable to *pediatrics*—the medicine of children, which has its own board examinations—but specialists in such fields as family practice and internal medicine are taking examinations given by the boards of those specialties to earn certificates of competence in geriatric medicine, and a subspecialty in geriatrics has been established in psychiatry.

Sheer numbers of people and vast amounts of money are behind these steps. One-third of health care spending in the United States is for the elderly, and the percentage is expected to increase as the number of old people grows. The chronic, disabling conditions common in older people are especially costly in human and financial terms, most tellingly when they lead to long-term institutionalization. In the 1980s, 40% of Medicaid spending went to pay for 1.5 million nursing home beds. Medicaid is a U.S. insurance plan intended to provide medical care for the poor. It is administered by the states but paid for in part by the federal government. Medicare is a corresponding insurance program for the elderly, but many older people's care is paid for by Medicaid because they have become medical paupers. The law requires them to spend almost everything they have on medical care before they receive Medicaid benefits. For many, turning to Medicaid is a last, desperate move.

One long-term hope is that many nursing home admissions can be prevented by providing better general care and preventive medicine programs tailored to the needs of older people. Toward that end, the National Institute on Aging has established a number of fellowships in geriatrics so that young doctors, teachers, and researchers can master the special requirements of geriatric medicine.

DISEASE AND THE ELDERLY

The special needs of older people start with the fact that they have a high incidence of disease. Younger people can have heart disease or diabetes or arthritis, but all these conditions are more likely to occur with age. Sometimes two or more of these chronic diseases afflict the same individual. A study by the National Center for Health Statistics in 1984 found that 46.5% of people over 64 had arthritis, compared to 5% of those under 45. The incidence of other conditions found in the study for the over-65 population was as follows: high blood pressure, 38%; hearing impairment, 28%; heart conditions, 27%; visual impairment, 13.6%. When one older person has several such conditions, medical care becomes more complicated.

In addition, some problems that are rare or minor in younger people become acute sources of trouble in later years. Some of them have already been mentioned, such as urinary incontinence, Alzheimer's disease, Parkinson's disease, and cataracts—all conditions that are relatively rare in the young but whose incidence rises rapidly with age. Ordinary falls, which seldom bother young people much, are a major concern of the elderly. In particular, broken hips and the complications that arise from them are a leading cause of nursing home entry and may even cause death in older people.

In today's aging population, more years translate into more disabling medical problems. The older people become, the sicker they are likely to get. The National Center for Health Statistics reports that 6.7% of people aged 65 to 74 require personal care assistance. That rises to 15.7% for those aged 75 to 84 and 44% at age 85 and older.

Dr. Robert Butler, who heads the Department of Geriatrics at Mount Sinai and was once director of the National Institute on Aging, points out that the U.S. medical care system is not designed for optimum treatment of chronic conditions. Its focus is acute illness, such as that caused by infections, whose time scale is measured in days or weeks and whose outcome is measured by cures. Chronic illness, requiring years of care and offering no hope of cure, just of relief, requires a different point of view. The new geriatrics fellowship programs are aimed at establishing that point of view in practicing physicians.

There is hope, however, that old age need not mean inevitable chronic illness. The Americans who are old today grew up in a different era, when times were tougher. The hope is that today's better diet, housing, and medical care will produce a generation of older Americans with fewer chronic ailments. And as noted throughout this book, there is a major research program to understand the basic mechanisms of such conditions as Alzheimer's disease, with the ultimate aim of prevention. Great success has already been achieved against stroke, one of the major cripplers of older people, through a combination of basic research and clinical medicine, whose major focus has been control of high blood pressure.

In the hope that the stroke success story can be repeated, more time and money is going into programs of preventive medicine aimed at other major ailments of the elderly. For example, the

Doctors are working to treat and/or prevent the injuries and diseases that often lead to institutionalization in a nursing home. Alzheimer's disease and falls resulting in broken bones are two such examples.

National Institute on Aging has helped establish a number of incontinence clinics throughout the country. These clinics are working to help older people control incontinence with such tools as exercise courses and *biofeedback*, a technique by which individuals gain some control over physiological functions by being given information about such functions. In another effort, a number of studies are being done to see if dietary changes, exercise, and other interventions can help prevent osteoporosis in older women. A related effort is a program to identify persons at high risk of falls and train them in preventive techniques. The combination of osteoporosis and a fall can be particularly dangerous, resulting in broken bones that cause institutionalization or death.

Many of the findings in these studies appear obvious: The incidence of falls is highest in individuals with multiple disabilities, and the danger is increased by poor lighting, by household hazards such as unanchored rugs, and by medications that affect the sense of balance. The important point is that research is being done, and the findings are being applied to reduce the risk of ailments common in old age.

MEDICATION AND THE ELDERLY

An accompanying effort of great importance centers on the use—and misuse—of medicine by the elderly. Older people take a lot of medications. They inevitably suffer more side effects. The over-all incidence of adverse drug reactions in the elderly is 2 or 3 times higher than in younger people, and anywhere from 10% to 30% of hospitalizations in elderly patients are for medication-related problems.

A root cause of these problems is the number and variety of medications taken by older people. Many of the elderly take prescription drugs for several chronic conditions: arthritis, heart disease, Parkinson's disease, and so on. Unexpected adverse side effects can occur from interactions between these drugs. Such interactions can happen at any age, but they are more probable in older people because they are more likely to have multiple prescriptions—sometimes from a number of doctors, because the elderly are likely to see several specialists.

Over-the-counter drugs can add to the problem of adverse interactions. A Canadian study done in 1986 found that almost two-thirds of older people took nonprescription drugs. More than half of the over-the-counter drugs reported in the survey were painkillers; 13% were cough and cold medicines. Only 1 patient in 12 had consulted a doctor about the use of nonprescription drugs.

Over-the-counter drugs can have side effects—a fact that becomes more important as a growing number of drugs once given only by prescription are made available for nonprescription use. Examples of drugs that no longer require prescriptions are the painkiller ibuprofen and the antihistamine diphenhydramine hydrochloride (trade name Benadryl). Ibuprofen can increase blood concentration of sodium, which can be a problem for a patient with congestive heart failure. Benadryl can interact with other drugs to cause confusion and even psychosis in some patients. Doctors who treat the elderly stress the need to do thorough questioning about medication use before another prescription is written.

The normal aging process also changes the way in which the body handles drugs. Those changes affect every aspect of a drug's effects, starting from the moment it enters the body. When a person swallows a drug, it goes first to the stomach and then to the intestine, where it is absorbed into the bloodstream. After absorption, the drug travels through the blood to the organ or tissue—heart, brain, joints, whatever—that is to be treated. But it also travels elsewhere in the body. The dose prescribed by a physician is intended to be just enough to achieve the desired effect on the target organ or tissue, with a minimum of adverse side effects on the other tissues that the drug reaches. That dose is based on normal distribution of the drug throughout the body.

Some of the drug will be carried to the liver, where it will undergo changes. One of the major functions of the liver is to metabolize substances that enter the body, changing them chem-

Many elderly people take several medications simultaneously. If extreme care is not taken, adverse reactions can occur. They can be caused by over-the-counter drugs as well as by prescription medications.

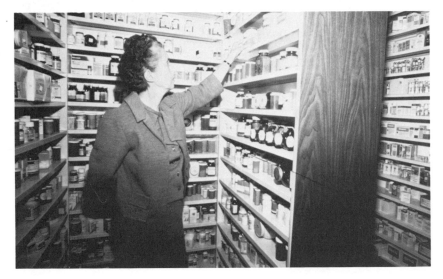

ically to meet the body's needs. As the drug passes through the liver, the processes that go on there can form metabolic products that have pharmacological activity. But in the long run, the liver will metabolize the drug more thoroughly, until it is completely inactivated. Metabolism in the liver is the main route of inactivation for many drugs.

Eventually, all of the drug will be metabolized. Many of the resulting waste products will be excreted from the body through the kidneys. Their role is to filter waste substances out of the blood and excrete them into the urine for disposal. The time needed for metabolism and excretion varies from drug to drug. Some disappear from the body within a few hours of being taken. Others can linger for weeks. Physicians often talk about the *half life* of a drug, the time in which half the original dose disappears from the body. The dose prescribed for an ailment often depends on the half life of a drug, which is based on human studies.

These studies are generally done on healthy younger individuals. It is only recently that researchers have begun to realize that doses calculated on the basis of these studies may not apply to older people because the old body handles many drugs differently than the young body. As a result, more older people are being included in the drug trials required by the Food and Drug Administration.

The effects of aging on drug metabolism start in the small intestine, where drugs are absorbed into the blood. A healthy digestive tract absorbs drugs just about as well in old age as in youth. The incidence of digestive disorders goes up with age, however, as does the possibility that drug absorption might be reduced.

Drug activity is also affected by changes in body composition. Most people experience a decrease in muscle mass and an increase in body fat as they grow older. The effects of increased fat content vary from drug to drug, depending on whether a specific drug is readily absorbed by fat. In some cases, more of the drug will reach the blood faster in old people than in the young. In other cases, drug activity will be prolonged because the half life is longer.

To complicate the matter further, the sensitivity of many tissues to drugs changes with age. As a rule, the aging body becomes more sensitive to extremes; for example, older people do not

Ideally, old age should be a time of relaxation and enjoyment rather than of hardship. Scientists and doctors are working on medical advances that will make this possible for more people.

adapt well to very high or very low temperatures. Individual organs—the heart, the liver, and so on—are also less adaptive. So even though a drug is absorbed with equal efficiency, the same dose may have a greater effect on an organ because of its increased sensitivity. The duration of its effects may also be changed because of alterations in half life.

The changes in the body's metabolism that occur with age also affect half life. The liver gets less blood with increasing age, and it shrinks somewhat, so many drugs are metabolized slower. It is common for doctors to prescribe smaller doses of these drugs for older people. But changes in the liver's metabolic ability do not occur in the same way in all older people, so it is necessary for doctors to monitor some drug doses carefully in the elderly to see whether an individual is experiencing diminished benefits or excessive side effects.

The kidneys also work less efficiently with age. As a rule, the kidneys of someone over 65 work about half as efficiently as they did in youth. But there is great individual variation in kidney efficiency with age, so it is common for doctors to order a test of kidney function when prescribing a drug that is disposed of primarily by the kidneys.

Doctors who treat old people are constantly cautioned to take careful drug histories, including over-the-counter medications, before writing a new prescription; to start with smaller doses and monitor the dosage continually; and to be alert for drug-induced illness and drug interactions.

The point of all these precautions is to make life easier for the elderly by proper use of medications. The fundamental aim of geriatric medicine is to make life better for the elderly by pre-venting disease when possible and treating it effectively when necessary. Modern medicine holds out the promise that the last years of life can be as full as the first. There should be no reason why older people cannot continue to be active, happy participants in all aspects of life. It is to be hoped that old age will come to be thought of as, and in fact be, more a time to enjoy than to fear.

•　　　•　　　•　　　•

PICTURE CREDITS

APPENDIX:
FOR MORE INFORMATION

The following is a list of organizations that can provide further information on aging and age-related disorders.

GENERAL

Aging in America
1500 Pelham Parkway South
Bronx, NY 10461
(212) 824-4004

American Association of Retired
    Persons (AARP)
National Gerontological Resource
    Center
1900 K Street NW
Washington, DC 20049
(202) 872-4700

American Geriatrics Society
770 Lexington Avenue
New York, NY 10021
(212) 308-1414

The Center for Social Gerontology
    (TCSG)
117 North First Street
Suite 204
Ann Arbor, MI 48104
(313) 665-1126

Center for the Study of Aging
706 Madison Avenue

Albany, NY 12208
(518) 465-6927

Department of Health and Human
    Services
Office of Information
300 Independence Avenue SW
Washington, DC 20201
(202) 619-0441

Elder Health Program
University of Maryland
School of Pharmacy
20 North Pine Street
Baltimore, MD 21201
(301) 328-3243

International Federation on Aging
Publication Division Office
1133 20th Street
Washington, DC 20049
(202) 662-4987

National Association of Agencies on
    Aging
600 Maryland Avenue SW
Suite 208
Washington, DC 20024
(202) 484-7520

National Association of State Units
  on Aging
2033 K Street NW
Suite 304
Washington, DC 20006
(202) 785-0707

National Council of Senior Citizens
925 15th Street NW
Washington, DC 20005
(202) 347-8800

National Council on Aging
Publications Department
600 Maryland Avenue SW
Washington, DC 20024
(202) 479-1200

National Institutes of Health
National Institute on Aging
Federal Building
Room 6C-12
9000 Rockville Pike
Bethesda, MD 20892
(301) 496-4000

AGE-RELATED DISORDERS

Alzheimer's Association
70 East Lake Street
Suite 600
Chicago, IL 60601
In the U.S.: (800) 621-0379
In Illinois: (800) 572-6037
or (312) 853-3060

Alzheimer Society of Canada
1320 Yonge Street
Suite 302
Toronto, Ontario M4T 1X2
(416) 925-3552

American Sleep Disorders
  Association
604 Second Street SW
Rochester, MN 55902
(507) 287-6006

American Society of Cataract and
  Refractive Surgery
3702 Pender Drive

Suite 250
Fairfax, VA 22030
(800) 451-1339

Better Hearing Institute
Box 1840
Washington, DC 20013
(703) 642-0580
Hearing Helpline:
(800) 424-8576

Better Sleep Council
P.O. Box 13
Washington, DC 20044
(703) 683-8371

Better Vision Institute
1800 North Kent Street
Suite 1210
Rosslyn, VA 22209
(703) 243-1528

Continence Restored
785 Park Avenue
New York, NY 10021
(212) 879-3131

Foundation for Glaucoma Research
490 Post Street
Suite 830
San Francisco, CA 91402
(415) 986-3162

National Institute for Neurological
  Disorders and Stroke (NINDS)
Building 31
Room 8A06
9000 Rockville Pike
Bethesda, MD 20892
(301) 496-5751

National Osteoporosis Foundation
2100 M Street NW
Suite 602
Washington, DC 20037
(202) 223-2226

Parkinson Foundation of Canada
55 Bloor Street West
Suite 232
Toronto, Ontario M4W 1A6
(416) 964-1155

FURTHER READING

GENERAL

Adelman, Richard C., and Eugene E. Dekker. *Modification of Proteins During Aging*. New York: Alan R. Liss, 1985.

Amoss, Pamela T., and Stevan Harrell. *Other Ways of Growing Old: Anthropological Perspectives*. Stanford: Stanford University Press, 1981.

Balin, Arthur K., and Albert M. Kligman, eds. *Aging and the Skin*. New York: Raven Press, 1988.

Barash, David P. *Aging: An Exploration*. Seattle: University of Washington Press, 1983.

Blau, Zena S., ed. *Current Perspectives on Aging and the Life Cycle*. Vol. 3. Greenwich, CT: Jai Press, 1988.

Craik, Fergus, and Sandra Trehub, eds. *Aging and Cognitive Processes*. New York: Plenum, 1982.

Henig, Robin M. *How a Woman Ages*. New York: Ballantine Books, 1985.

March, James, and James McGaugh, eds. *Aging: Biology and Behavior*. New York: Academic Press, 1981.

Neumann, James W. *Listening to Your Own Body: A Guide to the Neurological Problems That Afflict Us as We Grow Older*. Bethesda, MD: Adler & Adler, 1987.

Pesmen, Curtis, and Esquire Editors. *How a Man Ages*. New York: Ballantine Books, 1984.

DISEASE AND DYSFUNCTION

Alzheimer's Disease and Related Disorders Association Staff. *Understanding Alzheimer's Disease: What It Is, How to Treat It, How to Cope with It*. Edited by Miriam K. Aronson. New York: Scribners, 1988.

Arthritis Foundation Staff. *Understanding Arthritis: What It Is, How It's Treated, How to Cope with It.* New York: Scribners, 1985.

Bayles, Kathryn A., et al. *Communication and Cognition in Normal Aging and Dementia.* Boston: College-Hill Press, 1987.

Beck, William A., and Louis V. Avioli. *Osteoporosis.* Washington, DC: American Association of Retired Persons, 1988.

Davies, Peter, and Caleb E. Finch. *Molecular Neuropathology of Aging.* Cold Spring Harbor, NY: Cold Spring Harbor Laboratory, 1988.

Fischr, Abraham, ct al., eds. *Alzheimer's and Parkinson's Disease: Strategies for Research and Development.* New York: Plenum, 1986.

Janovic, Joseph, and Eduardo Tolosa. *Parkinson's Disease and Movement Disorders.* Baltimore: Urban & Schwartzenberg, 1988.

Johnson, Horton A., ed. *Relations Between Normal Aging and Disease.* New York: Raven Press, 1985.

Johnson, John E., Jr., et al. *Free Radicals, Aging and Degenerative Diseases.* New York: Alan R. Liss, 1986.

Maurer, James F., and Ralph R. Rupp. *Hearing and Aging: Tactics for Intervention.* New York: Grune & Stratton, 1979.

Rosenbloom, Alfred A., and Meredith Morgan. *Vision and Aging: General and Clinical Perspectives.* New York: Professional Press Books, 1986.

Sekular, Robert, et al. *Aging and Human Visual Functions.* New York: Alan R. Liss, 1982.

Tanagho, Emil A. *Contemporary Management of Impotence and Fertility.* Baltimore: Williams & Wilkins, 1988.

Van Toller, C., et al. *Ageing and the Sense of Smell.* Springfield, IL: Charles C. Thomas, 1985.

Yoshikawa, T. T., ed. *Aging and Infectious Diseases.* New York: S. Karger, 1984.

MEDICAL CARE

Dean, Ward. *Biological Aging Measurement: Clinical Applications.* 2nd ed., eds. Hans U. Weber, et al. Los Angeles: The Center for Bio-Gerontology, 1988.

Gaitz, C. M., and T. Samorajski, eds. *Aging Two Thousand: Our Health Care Destiny.* Vol. 1. New York: Springer-Verlag, 1985.

Regelson, William, and F. Marott Sinex. *Intervention in the Aging Process. Part B: Basic Research and Pre-Clinical Screening.* New York: Alan R. Liss, 1983.

Reichel, William. *Clinical Aspects of Aging.* Baltimore: Williams & Wilkins, 1988.

Scheff, Steven W., ed. *Aging and Recovery of Function in the Central Nervous System.* New York: Plenum, 1984.

Zarit, Steven H. *Aging and Mental Disorders: Psychological Approaches to Assessment and Treatment.* New York: Free Press, 1983.

NUTRITION AND EXERCISE

Harris, Raymond, and Sara Harris, eds. *Physical Activity, Aging and Sports.* Vol. 1, Scientific and Medical Aspects. Albany: The Center for the Study of Aging, 1988.

Hutchinson, Martha L., and Hamish N. Munro. *Nutrition and Aging.* New York: Academic Press, 1986.

Minirth, Frank B., et al. *Beating the Clock: A Guide to Maturing Successfully.* Grand Rapids, MI: Baker Book House, 1986.

Morse, Donald R., and Robert L. Pollack. *Nutrition, Stress and Aging: An Holistic Approach.* New York: AMS Press, 1987.

Pauling, Linus. *How to Live Longer and Feel Better.* New York: Avon Books, 1987. Schmerl, E. Fritz. *A Guide to Growing Older in Health and Happiness.* New York: Continuum, 1986.

Shepherd, Roy J. *Physical Activity and Aging.* Rockville, MD: Aspen, 1987.

Weindruck, Richard, and Roy L. Walford. *The Retardation of Aging and Disease by Dietary Restriction.* Springfield, IL: Charles C. Thomas, 1988.

Young, Eleanor A. *Nutrition, Aging and Health.* New York: Alan R. Liss, 1986.

GLOSSARY

acetylcholine a chemical that transmits signals between nerve cells; the blockage of the action of acetylcholine can impair the ability to retain new and recall old information, a symptom of Alzheimer's disease

AIDS acquired immune deficiency syndrome; a condition of acquired immunological deficiency caused by a virus (HIV) and spread by blood or sexual contact; usually recognized clinically by a life-threatening infection and a marked depression of the immune system

Alzheimer's disease a degenerative disease of the central nervous system characterized by premature mental deterioration

amyloid a starchy substance, containing protein fragments, that has been found in the tissues of patients with certain chronic disease states; found in the brain tissue of Alzheimer's patients

anosmic lacking the sense of smell

antioxidant chemical a substance that inhibits reactions promoted by oxygen

atrophy a wasting away or progressive decay

attrition a reduction in number

bacteria unicellular organisms lacking a distinct nuclear membrane; some cause diseases

basal ganglia a part of the brain that helps control body movement

benign prostatic hypertrophy enlargement of the prostate gland caused by the aging process rather than by infection or tumor

beta-carotene a form of vitamin A

biofeedback the technique of making unconscious or involuntary bodily processes, such as heartbeat or brain waves, perceptible to the senses by machinery in order to manipulate them by conscious mental control

brain stem the stemlike part of the brain that connects the brain to the spinal cord

calorie restriction a technique that involves limiting the food intake of an organism to the bare minimum in order to slow metabolism and thereby extend life span

carbohydrate a member of a group of compounds that share a general biochemical structure containing carbon, hydrogen, and oxygen; includes sugars and starch; must be obtained by people through diet

cardiac output the amount of blood pumped by the heart with each contraction

cataract a gradual clouding of the lens of the eye

cell the fundamental structural and functional unit of living organisms

centrophenoxine a drug used to prevent the accumulation of the pigment lipofuscin in the cells of the aged

chemosensory disorder disorders of the senses of smell and taste

climacteric the period that marks the end of a woman's reproductive period (female climacteric, or menopause); a corresponding period of lessening of sexual activity of the male (male climacteric)

clinical depression a disorder of the mind and nervous system marked by sadness, inactivity, difficulty in thinking and concentrating, changes in appetite and sleeping patterns, feelings of hopelessness, and sometimes suicidal tendencies

Creutzfeldt-Jakob disease a rare, usually fatal degenerative disease caused by the presence of a virus in the bloodstream

cross-linking theory the belief that aging results from chemical bonds between protein molecules

dementia a class of deteriorative mental disorders involving a general loss of intellectual abilities such as memory, judgment, and abstract thinking as well as noticeable changes in personality

dermatologist a doctor specializing in treatment of the skin

diabetic retinopathy a weakening of the retina caused by swelling and breaking blood vessels in the eye

DNA deoxyribonucleic acid; genetic material that contains the chemical instructions for determining an organism's inherited characteristics

dopamine a chemical that transmits signals between nerve cells; the depletion of the brain's supply of dopamine can cause muscular rigidity, stiffness, and trembling, symptoms characteristic of Parkinson's disease

Down's syndrome a genetic disease that causes moderate to severe mental retardation

eldepryl a monoamine oxidase inhibitor used in the treatment of Parkinson's disease

ergot alkaloid a drug related to those used for the treatment of migraine headaches

error catastrophe theory the belief that the malfunction of one protein from cumulative damage to the protein-making mechanisms can affect other proteins and ultimately result in the death of the organism

error theories a set of theories with the common foundation that aging is caused by the accumulated damage of mistakes and mutations in the essential machinery of life

estrogen a sex hormone produced in the ovaries of females and in the adrenal glands of both sexes

fluoridation the addition of stannous fluoride—a compound that helps prevent tooth decay—to drinking water

free radical theory the belief that highly unstable chemical fragments called free radicals, which are produced in metabolism, react with and degrade the functioning of essential molecules in the cell

genes complex units of chemical material that are responsible for inherited traits such as gender or eye color

geriatrics a branch of medicine that deals with the problems and diseases of old age and aging people

gerontology the scientific study of aging

glaucoma a disease of the eye, marked by pressure within the eyeball, that results in a gradual loss of vision

half-life the time required for half the amount of a substance, such as a drug introduced into the body, to disintegrate or be eliminated by natural processes

hormones products of living cells, hormones circulate freely in the bloodstream and produce a specific effect on cellular activity, regulating many bodily processes

hysterectomy surgical removal of the uterus

impotence the inability to have or maintain erection long enough to have sexual intercourse

incontinence the inability to regulate one's urination or defecation

insomnia the inability to obtain adequate sleep

L-dopa a compound drug that is the mainstay of treatment for Parkinson's disease

lipofuscin a dark brown pigment that accumulates in cells of the aged

macula an irregular, yellowish depression on the retina; its variation in size, shape, and coloring may be related to the different types of color vision

macular degeneration an eye condition of unknown cause that can result in blindness; it involves marked deterioration of the abilities of sharp-focus vision and color differentiation

malignant melanoma a darkly pigmented tumor; an often fatal cancerous condition caused by exposure to the ultraviolet radiation in sunlight

menopause the time in a woman's life when menstruation and the production of the female sex hormone estrogen stop

menstruation the monthly discharge of blood and cells from the lining of the uterus; occurs during the reproductive period of a woman's life

metabolic rate theory the belief that organisms with faster metabolisms have shorter life spans than those with slower metabolisms

metabolism the conversion of food and oxygen into energy that the body needs

migraine headache a recurrent severe headache often accompanied by nausea and vomiting

monoamine oxidase a chemical in the brain that plays a role in depression

monoamine oxidase inhibitors a class of antidepressant drugs

MPPP 1-methyl-4-phenyl-4-proprionoxypiperidine; a synthetic opiate related to heroin

multi-infarct dementia a form of dementia following a deteriorating course (a series of strokes) caused by the hardening of the arteries in the brain

nerve growth factor a substance normally produced in small amounts by the body, currently being tested for its ability to prevent the death of brain cells

oral abscess a pus-filled area in the mouth that can result from infection or neglected dental decay

osteoarthritis an inflammation of joints marked by degeneration of the cartilage and bone of these joints

osteoporosis a gradual thinning of the bones; afflicts more women than men and usually occurs after menopause

Parkinson's disease a progressive neurological disease of later life that is marked by a slowly spreading tremor, by muscular weakness and rigidity, and by a peculiar way of walking

pathology the study of the nature and cause of disease and the structural and functional changes caused by it; the condition produced by disease

pediatrics a branch of medicine dealing with the development, care, and diseases of children

periodontal disease a weakening of the gums, bones, and other structures that support teeth

plaques clusters of degenerating nerve cell endings

presbycusis age-related hearing loss

presbyopia the difficulty in focusing that accompanies the age-related loss of flexibility of the lens of the eye and muscles surrounding it

programming theories a set of theories commonly stating that aging is genetically instructed

rheumatoid arthritis a chronic disease characterized by pain, stiffness, inflammation, and sometimes destruction of joints

rickets a disease caused by deficiency of vitamin D, marked by soft and often deformed bones

saturated holding all that can be absorbed; a saturated compound, such as saturated fat, does not tend to unite directly with another compound

senile dementia dementia occurring in the aged

stapedectomy removal of the stapes bone from the ear; a treatment for conduction deafness

substantia nigra a layer of the brain containing dopamine-producing cells whose secretion tends to be deficient in Parkinson's disease

tangles masses of twisted nerve filaments that accumulate in nerve cells

testosterone a sex hormone produced in the testes of males and in the adrenal glands of both males and females

tinnitus a subjective sense of ringing in the ears

unsaturated capable of absorbing more of something; able to join chemically to other molecules, such as unsaturated fat

uterus a pear-shaped organ in a woman's reproductive system; during pregnancy a baby develops and is nourished there

virus a tiny acellular parasite composed of genetic material and a protein coat; the causative agent of some infectious diseases

wear and tear theory the belief that aging occurs because the efficiency of the body's repair mechanisms for DNA declines over the years

INDEX

Edward Edelson is science editor of the *New York Daily News* and past president of the National Association of Science Writers. His books include *The ABCs of Prescription Narcotics* and the textbook *Chemical Principles*. He has won awards for his writing from such groups as the American Heart Association, the American Cancer Society, the American Academy of Pediatrics, and the American Psychological Society.

Dale C. Garell, M.D., is medical director of California Children Services, Department of Health Services, County of Los Angeles. He is also associate dean for curriculum at the University of Southern California School of Medicine and clinical professor in the Department of Pediatrics & Family Medicine at the University of Southern California School of Medicine. From 1963 to 1974, he was medical director of the Division of Adolescent Medicine at Children's Hospital in Los Angeles. Dr. Garell has served as president of the Society for Adolescent Medicine, chairman of the youth committee of the American Academy of Pediatrics, and as a forum member of the White House Conference on Children (1970) and White House Conference on Youth (1971). He has also been a member of the editorial board of the *American Journal of Diseases of Children.*

C. Everett Koop, M.D., Sc.D., is former Surgeon General, Deputy Assistant Secretary for Health, and Director of the Office of International Health of the U.S. Public Health Service. A pediatric surgeon with an international reputation, he was previously surgeon-in-chief of Children's Hospital of Philadelphia and professor of pediatric surgery and pediatrics at the University of Pennsylvania. Dr. Koop is the author of more than 175 articles and books on the practice of medicine. He has served as surgery editor of the *Journal of Clinical Pediatrics* and editor-in-chief of the *Journal of Pediatric Surgery*, Dr. Koop has received nine honorary degrees and numerous other awards, including the Denis Brown Gold Medal of the British Association of Paediatric Surgeons, the William E. Ladd Gold Medal of the American Academy of Pediatrics, and the Copernicus Medal of the Surgical Society of Poland. He is a Chevalier of the French Legion of Honor and a member of the Royal College of Surgeons, London.